The evolution
and ecology of the
DINOSAURS

The evolution and ecology of the
DINOSAU

by L.B. Halstead

Illustrated by Giovanni Caselli

BOOK CLUB ASSOCIATES

LONDON

RS

Contents

Introduction

Dinosaurs are some of the most popular and familiar of all animals, yet they became extinct 64 million years ago, so no human being has ever seen one alive. The details of their life and times have fascinated us ever since the first remains were discovered and recognized 150 years ago. Today there is an increased interest, not just in their physical appearance, though this is startling enough, but in their behaviour and ecology.

The purpose of this book is to take a new look at the vast array of dinosaurs, in the light of the results of up-to-date research. Most people know something of the more spectacular dinosaur species, but few realize the number and variety that were alive during the 140 million years of their existence. Hundreds of different species have been discovered, though not all have complete skeletons. About some, scientists still know very little; for others there is considerably more information. As in all studies of the past, we build gradually upon known facts, looking at the logical ways the bones could have been used, comparing muscles and skeletons with those of modern reptiles, until we have a clear picture of what a dinosaur must have looked like and how it must have lived.

Many of the reconstructed scenes here are compiled from detailed studies made by scientists over a long period of time and they give as accurate a representation of the environment as is possible. Similarly, the new restorations of the dinosaurs have been made on the basis of the latest studies and discoveries and the theories based on them. Because they are up to date, some of the dinosaurs may look unfamiliar to readers who are used to the old-fashioned interpretations but these new illustrations, shown here for the first time, give a better idea of the tremendous variety of dinosaurs that evolved.

To appreciate the immense length of time the dinosaurs existed, it is worth considering how long man has lived on earth. In the 150 years since the first dinosaur bones were recognized as the remains of long-extinct giant reptiles, there have been some six generations – counting 25 years as a generation. There have been about 80 human generations in the years since the birth of Christ. Modern man, *Homo sapiens*, is believed to have been alive for about a quarter of a million years – that is for 10,000 generations – though his immediate ancestors can be traced back for about 3 million years, representing at least 120,000 generations. We know that some dinosaurs lived for about a hundred years and we can assume as a very conservative estimate that their generation period – the usual interval between the birth of a parent and its offspring – was also about 25 years. On this basis, from the origin of dinosaurs to their final extinction there must have been at least 5,500,000 generations. Even in the second half of the Cretaceous Period, when the duck-billed and horned dinosaurs evolved, there was time for 1,500,000 generations – more than ten times those in the entire

For J

This edition published 1977 by
BOOK CLUB ASSOCIATES
By arrangement with Eurobook Ltd

Copyright © 1975 by Eurobook Limited

ISBN 0 85654 018 8

Photoset by Tradespools Ltd, Frome, Somerset

Printed in Italy by Interlitho SpA

history and prehistory of man. Far distant in time though the Age of Dinosaurs seems, from its beginning to the present day is only one-twentieth of the history of the earth, which is believed to have originated in the solar system 4,500 million years ago!

During such a long period of time it is not really surprising that dinosaurs developed in size, shape and variety, though no one knows in detail why they evolved so spectacularly from small insect eaters no bigger than lizards to vast, 100 tonne giants. Changes like these usually occur very gradually as animals adapt to different environments. Most animals tend to become larger over the years: primitive horses, for example, were only the size of small dogs. The bigger an animal is, the fewer other animals can attack it, so the chances of survival for each large individual are increased and they are likely to produce more offspring. Similarly, an animal may, apparently by chance, evolve some feature that gives it an advantage over other animals of its own species. It may have a longer neck, for example, which enables it to find new food supplies – perhaps on the tops of trees. This means that it does not have to compete for food with all the other animals that share the lower leaves and grasses. If food becomes scarce because too many animals are using it, the long-necked ones will still have their own food supply and will be more likely to survive. When they breed, their offspring will inherit their advantages.

An alternative way of ensuring survival is to become very small and to reproduce very frequently, like mice or voles. Most larger animals do not bother to hunt such small prey and as their generation period is very short, probably a matter of weeks instead of years, inherited characteristics are quickly spread through the population.

The evolution of the dinosaurs, which continued right up to their extinction, was undoubtedly influenced by the major changes in the earth's surface and climate that took place during their time, but as yet we do not know all the answers.

The dinosaurs were not the only animals living and evolving during this time: they were just one group of egg-laying scaly reptiles, though they were by far the most important. Some of the animals that shared their world are included here so that the dinosaurs can be seen in the context of their times. Though they adapted to several different environments, they did not live in the sea and they did not fly. Marine reptiles and the pterosaurs, the so-called flying reptiles, took their places here; even small, furry mammals, distant forerunners of man, were living at the same time. Birds, too, evolved during the Age of Dinosaurs and it is the birds, the most successful of all flying vertebrates, that are their true descendants. Radically changed to suit a different world, the dinosaurs are, in a sense, alive today.

What is a dinosaur?

The dinosaurs were reptiles which dominated the earth for 140 million years. During this time the world they lived in changed in many ways. The continents drifted apart, the climate altered and plants evolved from simple forms to trees and flowering plants very like those we know today. The dinosaurs showed an enormous variety of adaptations to changing conditions and though they suddenly and mysteriously became extinct 64 million years ago, they were one of the greatest successes of past life. Their reign marks the high point of animal life on this planet.

To most people the remarkable thing about dinosaurs is their size. The largest were taller than a two-storey house and even the medium-sized species were twice the size of an elephant. Why did they grow to such enormous sizes, and what advantages did they gain?

It is very important for an animal to be able to keep the temperature inside its body at a constant level. If the temperature rises, all the internal processes such as breathing and digestion are speeded up. If the temperature cools, the processes are slowed down and the animal may not be able to function properly. Birds and mammals keep their temperature steady by increasing their metabolic rate, that is the rate at which their food is burnt to produce energy. The dinosaurs achieved the same condition in a unique way – they became giants.

As an animal becomes larger, it takes longer to cool down or warm up. The 30 tonne dinosaur *Apatosaurus*, for example, would have taken 84 hours – more than three days – to change its temperature 1 degree centigrade. The temperature inside a dinosaur's body was therefore amazingly constant and all its internal processes could take place at a steady rate, without sudden fluctuations. It was this mastery of their internal temperature that made the dinosaurs so successful for so long.

No-one has ever seen a dinosaur alive, for they became extinct more than 60 million years before the first man evolved. Until 150 years ago people did not even suspect that these strange reptiles had ever existed but now, after years of scientific study, we know a great deal about their life and times. Instead of imagining them as monsters of science fiction, it is possible to see them as real, living animals, perfectly adapted for life in the prehistoric world.

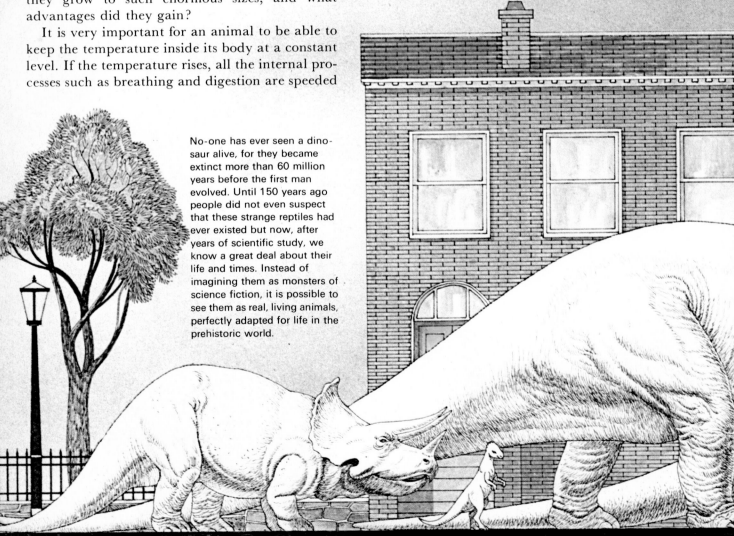

Triceratops　　　　　　*Stegoceras*　　　*Apatosaurus*

Pteranodon

Brachiosaurus   *Compsognathus*   *Tyrannosaurus*   11

GEOLOGICAL TIME

Geologists divide the thousands and millions of years that have passed since the world began into Eras. The Pre-Cambrian Era lasted 4,000 million years, and since then there have been three more: the Palaeozoic or Primary Era, the Mesozoic or Secondary Era and the Caenozoic Era which includes the Tertiary and the Quaternary in which we are now living. The Eras are divided into a number of shorter Periods, each lasting several million years. Some of the Periods are also divided into 'lower' (early) and 'upper' (late) sections.

Falling stars or meteorites, the moon and the earth are believed to be about 4,500 million years old and the oldest rocks known on earth have an age of between 3,900 and 3,700 million years. The very first signs of life are 3,200 million years old and consist of bacteria and simple one-celled plants, the blue-green algae. By 1,900 million years ago, many-celled plants were flourishing in the seas.

Animal life must have begun by this time but there is little sign of it until 680 million years ago. Then, around 570 million years ago, at the beginning of the Cambrian Period (the start of the Palaeozoic Era) many of the marine animals began to produce hard parts – shells and carapaces. From this point on a wealth of animal and plant material was preserved.

The ancestors of the vertebrates also left no record until they had evolved a bony armour, 500 million years ago, in the Ordovician Period. At the end of the Silurian, 410 million years ago, the first jawed fishes appeared and the first land plants. The Age of Fish, the Devonian Period, followed: insects appeared and, towards the end, the first amphibian.

Three hundred million years ago, in the middle of the Carboniferous Period (the Age of Amphibians) the first shelled egg was laid: the reptiles had arrived. But it was not until the Permian, 280 million years ago, that reptiles spread over the continents.

The Palaeozoic Era ended 225 million years ago and was followed by the Mesozoic. This Era, the Age of Dinosaurs, is divided into three parts. During the first, the Triassic, the dinosaurs began to evolve and become established. The middle period, the Jurassic, saw the greatest land animals ever known on earth. During the last, the Cretaceous, the dinosaurs adapted themselves to new types of plant food and evolved into many different forms. This was the climax of the Age of

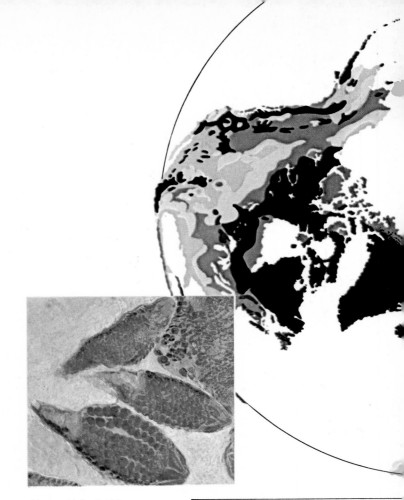

Above: *Holoptychius*, a primitive fish from the Palaeozoic Era, the Age of Fish. It was from lobe-finned fish like these that the first land vertebrates developed 345 million years ago.

Right: *Coelophysis*, a small, flesh-eating dinosaur from the Mesozoic Era, the Age of Reptiles. By the time *Coelophysis* evolved, around 200 million years ago, reptiles had become well adapted to life on land and some had become fast, active hunters.

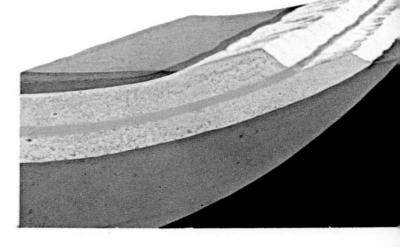

Right: There is very little record of life on earth until around 600 million years ago. If we think of the time since then as one hour, each minute on the clock equals 10 million years. The Palaeozoic Era lasted about 375 million years, the Mesozoic, which included the Age of Dinosaurs, for 161 million years and the Caenozoic for 64 million years. Man has only existed for about 3 million years — less than 20 seconds on the clock.

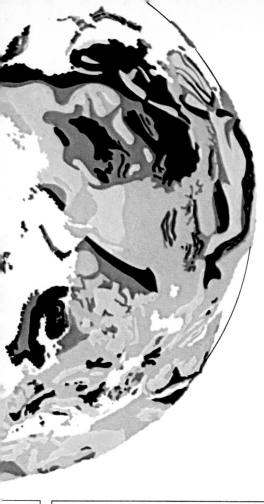

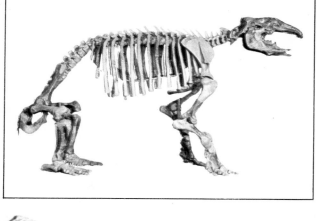

Left: *Palaeoparadoxia*, a sea cow from the Caenozoic Era, the Age of Mammals. After the Mesozoic, mammals became the dominant animals, some growing to giant forms unknown today.

Above: A human skeleton, over 2,000 years old, from the Quaternary Period, the Age of Man. Modern man, *Homo sapiens*, has existed for only about 225,000 years.

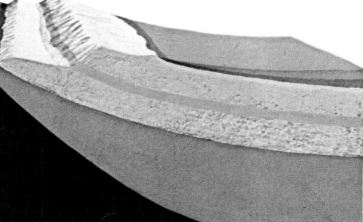

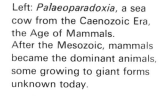

Fossil-bearing rocks are sandstones, limestones, clays and shales. The sediments that form them are laid down on top of one another but because of earth movements and erosion by wind and weather, rocks of all ages may appear at the surface, exposing fossils of animals that lived millions of years ago. The colours show rocks from the different geological Eras: Pre-Cambrian, more than 570 million years old (black); Palaeozoic, 570 to 225 million years old (grey); Mesozoic, 225 to 64 million years old (pink); and Caenozoic, less than 64 million years old (green). The map above shows where rocks of different ages appear on the surface today.

Dinosaurs. Then, quite suddenly, 64 million years ago they all vanished and the Tertiary Era, the Age of Mammals, began. About two million years ago the Quaternary Period, the Age of Man, began.

Dating The dating of rocks is done in two ways. One is the relative method, which uses the fact that when sands and muds are washed into the sea, the older ones are laid down first. From this it is possible to work out the relative ages of the sediments, though not actually how old they are. The second method involves analysing the radioactive materials in different types of rock. When radioactive substances give off radiations, they change at a fixed rate. For example, radioactive Uranium 238 slowly turns into a type of lead. Scientists can measure the rate of this change and from the amount of uranium and the amount of lead now in the rock, they can work out how many years it is since the rock was formed. Fossils found in the rock will be the same age as the rock itself. From this evidence it is now possible to pinpoint the actual years when many of the major events in the history of the world took place.

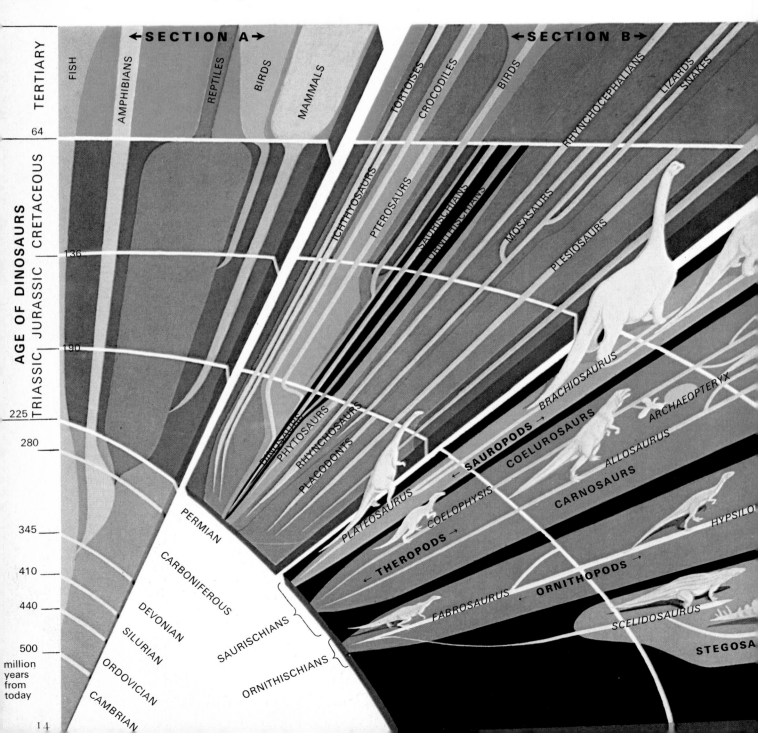

THE DINOSAURS' FAMILY TREE

Living things are divided into two basic kingdoms, the plants and the animals. The animal kingdom is divided again into a large number of distinct groups, each with its own special characteristics.

One of the most successful of these is the vertebrates, which are distinguished from other animals because they have a backbone and a cranium or brain-box. Today, there are five basic types of vertebrates. The most primitive type is the cold-blooded fish, which breathe through gills and swim by means of a muscular tail. Next come the amphibians. These are dual-purpose animals. The tadpoles spend their lives in water and breathe through gills, just like fish. When they grow older they change to an adult form, the gills disappear, lungs develop and they become land dwellers.

The third group, the reptiles, were the first vertebrates to live wholly on land. Their young do not live in the water but instead develop inside a closed egg. The development of this type of egg was probably the most important event in the history of the vertebrates.

The last two groups of living vertebrates are the warm-blooded birds and mammals, including man. Both these groups care for their young until they are able to fend for themselves.

The dinosaurs were reptiles – the most varied reptiles there have ever been. During the 140 million years they lived on earth, they changed and evolved into many hundreds of different species and spread into different environments all over the world.

All dinosaurs belonged to a group of reptiles called archosaurs. There were two separate types of dinosaur, the lizard-hipped dinosaurs (saurischians) and the bird-hipped dinosaurs (orni-

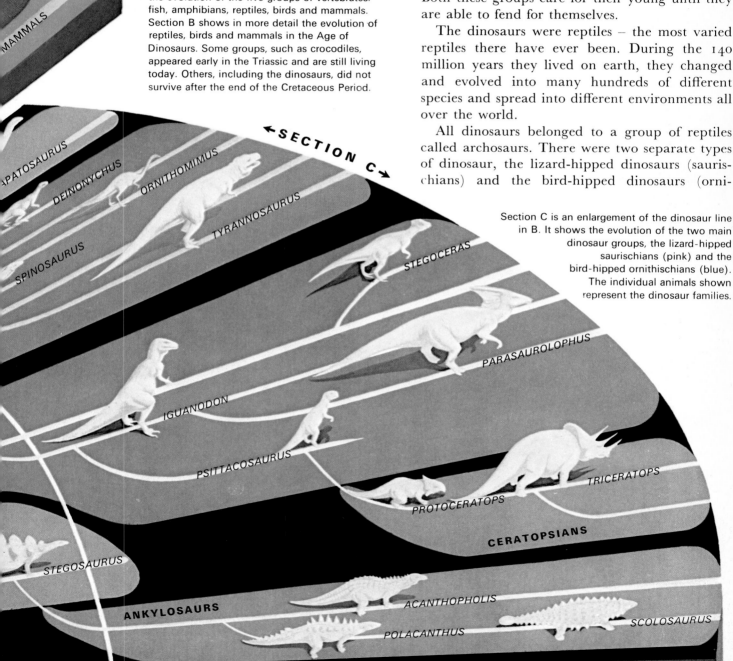

The evolution of the vertebrates. Section A shows the evolution of the five groups of vertebrates: fish, amphibians, reptiles, birds and mammals. Section B shows in more detail the evolution of reptiles, birds and mammals in the Age of Dinosaurs. Some groups, such as crocodiles, appeared early in the Triassic and are still living today. Others, including the dinosaurs, did not survive after the end of the Cretaceous Period.

Section C is an enlargement of the dinosaur line in B. It shows the evolution of the two main dinosaur groups, the lizard-hipped saurischians (pink) and the bird-hipped ornithischians (blue). The individual animals shown represent the dinosaur families.

MAMMALS

◄ SECTION C ►

APATOSAURUS
DEINONYCHUS
ORNITHOMIMUS
TYRANNOSAURUS
SPINOSAURUS
STEGOCERAS
IGUANODON
PARASAUROLOPHUS
PSITTACOSAURUS
PROTOCERATOPS
TRICERATOPS
CERATOPSIANS
STEGOSAURUS
ANKYLOSAURS
ACANTHOPHOLIS
POLACANTHUS
SCOLOSAURUS

thischians). Both these groups were again subdivided. The saurischians included the sauropods – gigantic plant-eating animals which lived partly in the water and walked on four legs when on land; and the theropods which lived on the land, walked on two legs and were flesh eaters.

The ornithischians were divided into four groups, the ornithopods, the ceratopsians, the stegosaurs and the ankylosaurs. All these were plant eaters.

The two-legged ornithopods were the first of the ornithischians. The ceratopsians, which evolved from them, walked on four legs and had horns and frills of bone on their heads. Stegosaurs and ankylosaurs also both walked on four legs and both developed thick, bony armour. Stegosaurs were covered in spiky points while ankylosaurs grew a thick covering, rather like the box-like carapace of a tortoise.

Today crocodiles are the only living archosaurs, but the archosaurs' descendants, the birds, are one of the most successful of all animal groups.

THE FOSSIL EVIDENCE

Our knowledge of the dinosaurs is based on the careful study of their fossilized remains preserved in rocks. The word 'fossil' originally meant any object that was dug up out of the ground but today it has come to mean only the preserved evidence of past life.

Some fossils are animal bones which have been petrified or turned to stone. Others are simply the shape and impression left by an animal's body after it has rotted away. Normally only animals with hard parts such as shellfish and vertebrates with their bones and teeth stand much chance of being preserved, though sometimes softer animals and plants survive. Even animals with hard parts must be buried shortly after death, for otherwise rain and wind will destroy them completely.

In order to be buried the body of the animal must finally come to rest in a place where sands and muds will cover it up. Lakes, rivers, coastal lagoons and swamps are ideal areas in which animals can be preserved but deserts and caves as well as sea shores also provide suitable conditions.

The hills and mountains and most of the land surface are gradually being worn away so that animals living and dying there are only rarely preserved. Fossils therefore give a rather misleading impression of animal life long ago. More animals that lived in or near the good preservation areas survive as fossils than any others and so they seem more important than perhaps they really were. Only occasionally an odd glimpse is given of the great variety of life that existed.

Even when the chances of being buried are good, there are still many hazards to be overcome before a fossil can be discovered. The sands and mud that buried it will, over the years, have been pressed together into rock. First, this rock must be raised to the surface by some movement of the earth so that wind and rain can gradually wear it away. Only then will there be any chance of the fossil being uncovered. If the fossil is exposed for too long, however, it will be destroyed by wind and rain. It must be discovered soon after parts of it are first exposed and the person who discovers it must recognize what he has found and alert the nearest museum so that they can organize a carefully-planned scientific excavation to recover the skeleton. If the discoverer tries to dig a large fossil out by himself, he may easily destroy valuable evidence without knowing it.

Bones and teeth are made up of the mineral apatite, calcium phosphate, together with a fibrous protein called collagen. The mineral part is easy to preserve and, surprisingly, even the protein part can survive as it is protected by the mineral. In some cases once the bones have been buried in sand, water seeping through dissolves away the bone, leaving only the shape where it has been. Some fossil reptiles are preserved in this way, and only an expert can recognize them. At first sight, they look simply like holes in the rock but when the holes are filled with rubber or plastic, a replica of the original bone can be produced. Working with materials like these is very difficult and needs hours of patience. Sometimes the natural moulds may be filled with some other mineral. In Australia reptile bones have been found replaced with precious opal.

The shape of bones may alter as they become fossilized. Sometimes they undergo a change called plastic deformation. This is a very slow process which makes the bone look as if it has been partly melted. More often the weight of the sediments that buried the skeleton simply crushes the bones flat. It is always necessary to be able to work out exactly what has happened to the bone since the animal died, as otherwise mistakes will be made.

An enormous amount of information about a dinosaur's way of life can be found from its bones and teeth alone. Fortunately, however, there are other types of dinosaur fossil which help to complete the picture. In several cases dinosaurs have

Fossils of many different kinds help to show what dinosaurs looked like when they were alive.

Above: The pattern of an *Iguanodon's* skin, made when it sat down in a sandy hollow over 100 million years ago.

Above, left: The complete skeleton of a small dinosaur, *Gallimimus*, embedded in rock.

Far left: Tracks of three flesh-eating dinosaurs found at Swanage, England. The footprints prove that these dinosaurs walked on their back legs, taking very small steps for their size and holding their tail clear of the ground.

Left: The skull of a bone-headed dinosaur from Mongolia, partly freed from its rocky surround. Complete skulls, with jaws and teeth, tell a great deal about a dinosaur's way of life.

died in an arid region and have been mummified in the dry heat before being covered by wind-blown sand. The sand has taken up the finest details of the texture of the skin so that we can see exactly what it looked like. One skin impression comes from a sandy hollow where a dinosaur sat down. In other places impressions of feathers of primitive birds or of the down or fur on flying reptiles make it possible to see exactly what these strange animals really looked like.

The brains of dinosaurs can be studied by making casts of the inside of the brain case and marks on fossilized bones often show where muscles have been. By studying individual bones and joints, scientists can tell how the animal moved and how big it must have been. An expert can discover a great deal from even a single bone.

If we want to imagine exactly what a dinosaur looked like when it was alive, some of the most valuable fossils are footprints. Trackways of footprints have been found in many parts of the world and they show exactly how the animals stood and walked, whether they had toes or webbed feet and whether their tail dragged on the ground.

We can even discover what a dinosaur ate from fossils. The structure of its teeth shows whether it ate plants or meat; smooth, rounded pebbles found in the ribcage mean that it swallowed stones to help grind and digest its food; sometimes even stomach contents are preserved. Fossil droppings, called coprolites, can also be studied but here it is not easy to tell exactly which dinosaur dropped which dropping.

The other aspect of dinosaur life for which there is firm evidence is the fact that they laid eggs – for the eggs themselves are preserved. Even the enormous swamp dwellers, weighing as much as 80 tonnes, came onto land to lay their eggs. By contrast some of the marine reptiles gave birth to live young and fossils are known which show that the mother died as she was giving birth, for mother and baby are preserved together.

Finally, by examining the microscopic structure of the bones, it is possible to record the injuries that one dinosaur gave another and the diseases from which they suffered. Osteoarthritis, a disease of the joints which old people get today, affected the dinosaurs and other animals of the time.

By taking all this evidence into account, we can build a comprehensive picture of the life of the dinosaurs, a picture which is based on factual evidence and does not rely on the imagination.

RECONSTRUCTING A DINOSAUR

The first discoveries of dinosaur remains were made in England at the beginning of the last century. Until that time, no-one had any idea that such giant creatures had ever existed. The flesh eater *Megalosaurus* was the first dinosaur to be found. It was excavated out of the Stonesfield slate quarry in Oxfordshire in 1822. In the same year the giant plant eater *Iguanodon* was discovered in a sandstone quarry near Cuckfield in Sussex. It was not until the second half of the nineteenth century that two Americans, Edward Drinker Cope and Othniel Charles Marsh found large numbers of dinosaur fossils in Colorado. Complete skeletons of such famous dinosaurs as *Triceratops, Stegosaurus, Diplodocus* and *Tyrannosaurus* proved beyond question that a race of giant reptiles had existed.

From the initial recognition of a piece of bone sticking out of the ground to the final life-like restoration involves an enormous amount of effort by teams of workers. Today the discovery of dinosaurs seems to be in the most remote and desolate parts of the earth and to begin with, an expedition has to be adequately equipped. It needs sturdy vehicles to negotiate the harsh conditions of the deserts, food and water, tools for excavating, chemicals for coating the surface of the bones when they are uncovered, bandages and plaster of Paris to protect them, tackle for lifting and wood for the construction of crates to carry the skeletons home.

Even when an expedition reaches its destination, dinosaur skeletons all too frequently occur in the most inaccessible places, such as half way up a cliff. When this happens scaffolding has to be constructed before the excavation can begin.

The first task is carefully to expose the bones by removing the sandstone or mudstone from around them. At this stage an accurate plan is made of the position of the bones, and each one is numbered.

As the bones are heavy it is not possible simply to dig them out and pack them into wooden boxes. They have to be specially prepared. First they are covered with wet paper, then strips of cloth are dipped in plaster of Paris and the bones are bandaged. Next the specimen is walled in by wooden planks, and plaster is poured into the crate. When it is filled and set solid, the box is undercut and turned over; the top and bottom are nailed on and the fossil bone, set in plaster and completely encased in its individual wooden crate, is loaded onto a lorry, to be transported many thousands of kilometres back to the laboratory.

Back in the museum, the reverse process takes place. The crate is removed and then the plaster until eventually, after months of careful chiselling, the fossilized bones are once more exposed.

At this stage the scientist begins his detailed examination of the specimen. The bones are measured and each one is carefully described. The roughened patches which show where the muscles were attached are studied. When the work is done, the scientist publishes a special book about it called a monograph. This contains photographs and drawings from different angles of all the individual bones. It also discusses the way in which the skeleton must have fitted together. The key evidence for this is the plan which was drawn up when the bones were first found. If the skeleton was complete and undisturbed this field plan will show how the dinosaur should be reconstructed.

By examining the various joints and bones it is possible to work out the types of movement the dinosaur could have made. Obviously size is important here. For example an animal that weighed several tonnes and had only minute front limbs must have walked on two legs, but it could certainly not have leaped about like a kangaroo.

Once this detailed scientific study has been completed, the museum or institute can either put the individual bones into store, or place them on view for the public. There are two ways of displaying the bones. They can be reassembled exactly as they were found in the rock. (This can only be done if an accurate plan was made at the time of the discovery.) Or the skeleton can be put together in a life pose. In this case a steel supporting framework must be made which will bear the weight of the fossil bones – often weighing several tonnes – but which will not be too obvious when it is in place. From organizing an expedition to the final public display may take several years.

Until the detailed scientific papers have been published the new dinosaurs have no names. It is only when they have been described that they can be identified as known dinosaurs, close relatives of known dinosaurs or as entirely new forms never found before. The joint Mongolian–Polish expeditions to the Gobi desert in the early 1970s found many dinosaurs quite new to science and each year new discoveries are made in many parts of the world. Recently the largest flying animal, with a wing span of 15 m, was announced – to the complete astonishment of all the experts. There are likely to be further surprises in the future.

In the nineteenth century, dinosaurs were found in many parts of Europe and the United States. Today most discoveries are made in more remote parts of the world. In the early 1970s Poland and Mongolia organized a joint expedition to the Gobi Desert, hundreds of kilometres from the nearest large town.

Above: The camp site at Khulsan in the Nemegt valley, Mongolia.

Above, left: Each bone is wrapped in plaster bandages, packed separately in a crate and firmly set in plaster of Paris to prevent damage on the journey home.

Above, far left: The skeleton of a large ankylosaur was found in rock half-way up a cliff face. Scaffolding had to be built before it could be excavated.

Left: Uncovering the skeleton of a large, plant-eating dinosaur, *Saurolophus*. Though the outer layers of rock can be removed with picks and shovels, the bones may be fragile and great care is taken as they are finally uncovered.

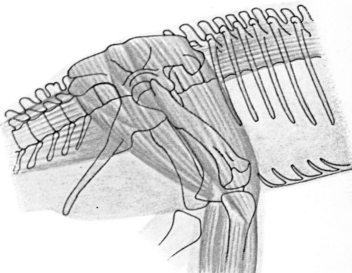

Scars on fossil bones show where muscles were once attached. By studying these and comparing them with muscles of living reptiles, it is possible to build up an accurate picture of a dinosaur's body and to work out what each part could do.

Left: Mounted skeleton of *Plateosaurus*, a 200 million year old plant-eating dinosaur. As the fossil bones are separate, they have to be fixed carefully in position and supported on a complicated steel scaffolding. Fine wires attached to its head, neck and tail give the dinosaur a realistic pose.

The origin of reptiles

FROM WATER TO LAND

The ancestry of the dinosaurs and of all land-living vertebrates can be traced back to extinct lobe-finned fishes which lived 380 million years ago.

One of the most important advances in the history of the vertebrates was their transition from water to land as gradually, over millions of years, fish evolved into amphibians and amphibians evolved into reptiles. In order to understand the changes that took place it is necessary to look at how these early fish lived and why they had to change in order to survive.

During the Devonian Period the fishes which had originated in the sea invaded the fresh water of lakes and rivers. We know from the sediments in which the fossils are preserved that the climate was sub-tropical with dry and rainy seasons, very like the climate of the savannah regions today. The seasonal drought is a critical period for fish as the rivers and lakes dry up and only small ponds are left. Fish breathe by means of gills and they obtain the oxygen they need from the water. As the ponds dried up in the sun, the remaining water became fouled – all the oxygen it contained was used up.

Though the oxygen in the water was gone, there was still plenty of oxygen in the air all around, produced by the early land plants. Any fish that could exploit this new source stood a much better chance of surviving and almost all the different kinds of freshwater fishes developed extra breathing organs to do just this. These organs were the beginnings of lungs and at first they simply enabled the fish to survive as fish. There was certainly no incentive for the fish to move onto land.

If a fish is trapped in an isolated small pond and the pond begins to dry out completely, survival will not simply be a question of breathing air, but also of having food and of keeping the skin moist. There are two possible solutions. The fish can bury itself in the mud and protect itself by secreting a cocoon of mucus (as the lungfish does today) and sleep through the hot, dry season. This is called aestivating. Or it can leave the shrinking pond and crawl across the mud until it reaches another, larger one.

A fish could only crawl if its fins were muscular, with a strong bony skeleton inside. Three groups of fish developed fins like these, the lungfish, the coelacanths and the rhipidistians. The bones of their fins foreshadow the bones in the limbs of land-living vertebrates and represent the second evolutionary stage in the slow journey from water to land.

Paired fins like this did not, however, originate to enable fish to move onto land, but to enable them to move more freely in the water. At first the fins were broad-based triangles which could not move very much and were used to balance the fish in the water. Gradually fish became better swimmers and as they became more manoeuvrable, the base of the fin narrowed and the bony parts, called radials, fused together. The fins de-

The stages of evolution from fish to reptile. *Eusthenopteron* was a lobe-finned fish living in the Devonian Period, 380 million years ago. It had developed primitive lungs and strong, muscular fins which enabled it to crawl for short distances over the land.

345 million years ago the first amphibian appeared. *Ichthyostega* was able to live both on land and in the water. It still lived the life of a fish and had a fish-like tail but its fins had changed into front and back legs with 5 fingers and toes.

veloped into two main types, the ray fins now seen in herring and salmon and the lobe fins. It is from the lobe fins, in a group called the bony fishes, that limbs eventually evolved.

At the end of the Devonian Period 345 million years ago, the first land vertebrate, *Ichthyostega*, appeared. This animal had powerful legs but it still kept its fish-like tail. The skull bones had also changed: its snout was longer and the back of its head shorter. This happened because a sense of smell is more important out of water than in it. Chemicals in the air are much weaker than they are in water, and in order to be able to detect them the smelling organs in the nose and the front of the brain must be more sensitive.

Ichthyostega is classified as an amphibian yet its

During the Carboniferous Period, amphibians became better adapted to the land, with less fish-like tails and stronger limbs. *Gephyrostegus* could live on land or in the water. It laid its eggs in water, where its tadpoles developed.

Above: *Seymouria baylorensis* shows a half-way stage between amphibians and reptiles. This skeleton, found in Texas, is over 250 million years old.

280 million years ago the reptiles appeared. *Hylonomus* lived most of its life in the water, but laid its shelled eggs on land.

way of life was entirely fishy. For the conditions of the time it was a very well-adapted fish and it used its ability to move over the land simply to give it a better chance of surviving the dry season. It is only because we know that it was the ancestor of the land vertebrates that its land features are so important.

The Carboniferous Period which followed the Devonian brought an important climatic change, with heavy rain all the year round. Extensive swamps now spread over vast areas of the continents. The shallow water, mud and fallen tree trunks provided an environment that suited the amphibians perfectly. Many became specially adapted for swimming in shallow water, and developed flattened bodies. The animals that still resembled the early fish-like amphibians spent longer on the drier parts of the swamp, feeding on insects and on other amphibians. Their fish-like tail vanished completely and the backbone developed extra joints, strengthening it so that it would not sag under the weight of the body.

The next evolutionary stage was the gradual change from amphibian to reptile. In parts of the swamps hollow rotten tree stumps formed animal traps and it is from these that fossils of the very first true reptiles have been recovered.

The only way of distinguishing a reptile from an amphibian is by its method of reproduction. Amphibians normally lay their eggs in water and the tadpoles swim and breathe in a fish-like way. In contrast to this, reptiles lay shelled eggs on land and the early development takes place in the egg.

The origin of the shelled egg was one of the most fundamental and far-reaching events in the history of the vertebrates. It meant that they no longer had to return to the water to breed and it made it possible for them to spread over the continents: without it the land would not have been conquered.

THE FIRST SHELLED EGGS

Though the vertebrates were now equipped to move onto dry land, surprisingly, they did not at first do so. The animals that evolved this new means of reproduction lived in the Carboniferous swamps. Here there was food in abundance while on land there was little to eat apart from plants. None of the vertebrates of this time was able to deal with vegetable matter: they ate one another, the smallest feeding on insects and worms. As there was certainly no incentive for them to leave the swamps and marshes, this can only mean that the

shelled egg, like the fish's bony fin, developed for some quite different reason. In this case also it was a question of survival.

There are two ways of ensuring the survival of offspring. One is to produce as many eggs as possible in the hope that at least some of them will develop safely. The other is to produce fewer but to allow them to develop in a protected and hidden environment, away from most other animals. The Carboniferous amphibians laid their eggs in water and they had to produce enormous numbers because, once laid, the eggs were at the mercy of all the other swamp dwellers. Even when the tadpoles hatched they would be eaten by insects and fish as well as by other amphibians. In laying their eggs on dry land the new 'super amphibians' evolved the second method of ensuring the survival of their young. No longer did the parents need to produce millions of eggs; a few, well hidden in the undergrowth near the water, were safe from predators and stood a good chance of hatching successfully.

The large-yolked eggs that began to be laid during the Carboniferous are called amniotic eggs because the young animals, called embryos, were covered in a sheet of tissue called the amniotic membrane. Inside this membrane was a safe, watery environment in which the embryos developed. A further sheet of tissue called the allantois, acted as a breathing organ, allowing the embryo to take in oxygen from the air outside and to get rid of carbon dioxide. Finally, everything was enclosed in a protective covering called the chorion.

An animal that produced an egg of this type is now classified as a reptile, even if it is living the life of an amphibian, partly on land and partly in the water. In the Carboniferous, they would simply have seemed especially successful, well-adapted amphibians. When the swamps dried up and most of the typical amphibians died out, it was the animals that laid amniotic eggs that survived.

The first fossil eggs are found in the Permian rocks, but there is no evidence yet to tell us which particular group of reptile produced them. When the dinosaurs were first described it was assumed that they laid eggs like other reptiles, but there was no proof until the beginning of this century when the American Museum of Natural History expedition to Central Asia discovered nests of fossilized eggs in the Gobi desert. The recent Polish–Mongolian expeditions also discovered such nests of eggs. The eggs are oval and are found in groups of 30, arranged in circles. The mother dino-

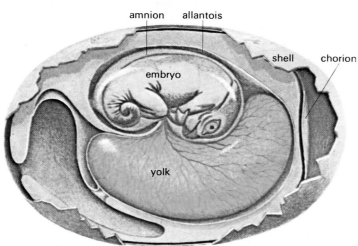

The shelled egg provided a safe, private pond for the embryo dinosaur. Enclosed by the amniotic membrane, it had everything it needed. Food was supplied by a nutritious yolk, while the allantoic membrane acted as a lung for breathing. The developing embryo was protected by the chorion and by the porous eggshell which also supplied mineral for its bones.

Baby *Protoceratops* dinosaurs breaking from their shells. A fully-grown *Protoceratops* measured 2 m, but the eggs it hatched from were no more than 7 cm across. (Brit. Mus. model)

Fossil eggs laid by a giant sauropod dinosaur. Each egg measures 20 cm across. Adult sauropods grew to 28 m long.

The outer surface of a sauropod egg, showing the thickness of the shell and the pattern of tiny pimples. Some dinosaur eggs contain fossilized young, but this broken egg was full of sand.

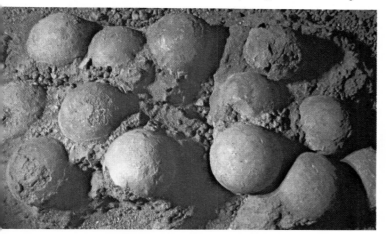

saur would have moved her egg-laying organ round so that each egg came to rest alongside the others. When the batch was complete, she would have covered the eggs up by scooping sand over them. This would have kept them warm and would also have hidden them from possible predators.

We know that the Mongolian eggs belonged to the horned dinosaur *Protoceratops* because several of the eggs contained the bones of baby dinosaurs that had died just before their time of hatching. Other kinds of eggs are known. Some large, round eggs found in the south of France belonged to giant plant-eating sauropod dinosaurs and had a volume of about 5 litres.

The shells of the eggs vary as well as their shapes. Under the microscope it is possible to see that the structure of the shell is different but even the outer surfaces have different textures. The large sauropod eggs have minute, rounded pimples on their surface, while the *Protoceratops* eggs have a series of irregular lines and grooves.

We only have a fossil record of eggs because they had a shell made up of the mineral calcium carbonate – the substance of which limestone is composed. In fact a hard shell like this is not a fundamental feature of the amniotic egg and several living reptiles have leathery shells with very little calcium carbonate in them.

When an egg is laid, the embryo is in a separate, closed world. The only thing it receives from outside is air. All the substances it needs to develop must therefore be provided in the egg itself. One of the most important of these is mineral, to build up the embryo's bones.

A strong, internal bony scaffolding has been the key to the success of the vertebrates and without it the dinosaurs would certainly never have existed. To produce its skeleton, the embryo needs large amounts of calcium and these are provided by the mother in the form of the eggshell. When the embryo begins to breathe oxygen it produces carbon dioxide as a waste product. The carbon dioxide reacts with the calcium carbonate in the shell to produce a substance called calcium bicarbonate. This dissolves, is absorbed into the blood supply of the allantois membrane and carried to the embryo to be used in its skeleton.

As the embryo grows the shell gradually becomes thinner and by the time it hatches it can break out quite easily. Some of the dinosaur eggs that have been found seem to have excessively thick shells. This is because they were not ready for hatching when the embryo died. If the baby dinosaur had developed fully, it would have used more of the calcium carbonate and the shell would have been thinner.

There are a few cases of extra thick dinosaur eggs, apparently caused by a disease suffered by the mother. These eggs have an extra layer of shell so that the minute pore spaces which normally allow air to pass to and fro are blocked. The embryo could not breathe but even if it could, it would never have been able to break through the double-thick shells. The same disease affects poultry today and some people have suggested that it may have contributed to the extinction of the dinosaurs.

THE CONQUEST OF THE LAND

At the end of the Carboniferous Period, 280 million years ago, the climate became drier again and the swamps disappeared. Many of the amphibians could not adapt to the new, harsher conditions but the animals that laid shelled eggs on land were able to survive and during the Permian (280 to 225 million years ago) the first major spread of true land-living animals began. Once on land permanently, they had to make further adaptations to cope with the new environment.

The swamp-living amphibians and reptiles fed on fish and other water animals, so their teeth and jaws only had to be able to trap food and prevent it from escaping from their mouths. On land the situation was very different. Here all the reptiles were flesh eaters of one kind or another, for no plant eaters had so far evolved. The reptiles all fed on one another, and as this involved fights and struggles, their jaws had to be strengthened so that they could grip and tear. The position of the bones in the jaw and skull changed and the jaw muscles became larger and more powerful.

Another important change that now took place was in the way animals stood and walked. Instead of sprawling on the ground as the early reptiles had done, their legs grew straighter and moved under the body. They could take longer strides because they moved from the shoulder and hip instead of from the elbow and the knee, and this helped them to run faster over the ground.

The reptiles that dominated the land at this time were primitive mammal-like reptiles or paramammals, called pelycosaurs. They were still cold

Before the dinosaurs evolved, mammal-like reptiles or paramammals had dominated life on land for over 70 million years. The large, primitive paramammals *Dimetrodon* and *Edaphosaurus* had sails over their backs which helped them to control their internal temperatures. Smaller paramammals such as *Ophiacodon* did the same thing by gradually speeding up their metabolic rate — the rate at which they burned up their food to produce heat and energy.

Edaphosaurus

Dimetrodon

Ophiacodon

blooded like the reptiles but *Dimetrodon*, a flesh eater, and *Edaphosaurus*, which probably ate molluscs, developed large sails running down their backs which helped them to control their temperature. The sails were supported by long spikes growing from the backbone and were covered in skin. When it was cold in the early morning the animal turned the sail to the sun and quickly warmed up. During the heat of the day, if the animal faced into the sun, only the thin edge of the sail would be directly exposed and the rest of its body could cool down.

The carnivore, *Dimetrodon*, was about 3·5 m long and weighed 250 kg. Without a sail it would have taken between 100 and 200 minutes to raise its temperature 6°C. In fact it took only about 50 minutes. The average *Dimetrodon* took 64 minutes to warm up to its daytime temperature, and the mollusc eater *Edaphosaurus* took 69 minutes. Only the larger animals seem to have needed this kind of temperature control mechanism: a smaller one from the same time, *Ophiacodon*, which weighed between 30 and 50 kg, never has a sail at all.

This strange sail was probably the first step towards warm-bloodedness but it was not until much later, towards the end of the Permian, that the paramammals finally became warm-blooded animals. Like birds and mammals today, they kept the temperature inside their bodies high by burning their food more quickly – a process called a high metabolic rate. To do this they needed a constant supply of oxygen and they developed a bony palate which separated their food and air passages so that they could breathe through the nose while they ate. This meant that they could hold food in their mouths for longer, preparing it for digestion.

Their teeth changed, too, developing special shapes for grasping food (incisors), for stabbing and tearing (canines) and for grinding (molars).

On the sides of the snouts of these later paramammals there were special pits where whiskers grew. From these, scientists believe that the animals were also covered in fur. This would have helped to keep their body temperature steady by insulating them from changes outside.

The paramammals dominated life on earth throughout the Permian and the early part of the next Period, the Triassic, evolving into many different forms. The first plant-eating paramammals, the dicynodonts, developed early in the Permian. They had a single pair of tusk-like teeth in their upper jaw and no other teeth at all. They were preyed on by several different kinds of flesh eaters, some with enormous stabbing and slashing teeth. By the beginning of the Triassic, 225 million years ago, the pattern of feeding, called the food chain, had become very like today's: most of the animals were plant eaters, while the few flesh eaters now ate them instead of one another.

The great spread of the paramammals marked the final conquest of the land and ended in the evolution of the true mammals. It was at this point that dinosaurs appeared. The consequences were dramatic. As the dinosaurs became successful all the paramammals disappeared. The only survivors of the struggle were small, warm-blooded mammals which managed to find a safe way of life by being active only at dusk and during the night.

Although the dinosaurs dominated the continents for 140 million years, throughout this vast period of time the nights belonged to the mammals.

Later paramammals, such as *Lycaenops*, were still scaly like other reptiles but their legs had changed so that they now walked high off the ground. Later still, paramammals like *Thrinaxodon* lost their scales, grew fur and developed ears. In most ways these later forms were almost true mammals but

it is thought that they probably still laid eggs like reptiles. The first real mammals were tiny, the size of rats and mice. When the paramammals became extinct, they survived. They were the first animals to suckle their young and it is from them that the world's mammals, including man, eventually evolved.

Lycaenops

Thrinaxodon

Morganucodon

The Triassic Period–225 to 190 million years ago

The Triassic Period, which marked the beginning of the Age of Dinosaurs, was a period of remarkable change. The ice cap that had covered part of the southern continents at the beginning of the preceding Permian Period, making life difficult for any reptile, had finally vanished; the climate had become more equitable, with semi-tropical conditions reaching almost to the poles. Many new groups of reptiles now appeared and colonized many new environments. The land-dwelling vertebrates flourished and spread over all the continents. That is, their remains are today found on every continent, for during the Triassic there was only one super-continent, Pangea.

Pangea consisted of two major land masses, a southern one called Gondwanaland and a northern one, Laurasia. Gondwanaland included present-day South America, Africa, India, Antarctica and Australia, with parts of the Middle East and Italy. Laurasia included North America, Europe and Asia. The two vast continents were linked where South and North America joined what is now the western bulge of Africa. Elsewhere they were divided by the great ocean of Tethys.

At the beginning of the Triassic, the paramammals still dominated life on earth. There were stoutly-built flesh eaters, herds of large plant eaters and small, furry lizard eaters. One successful plant-eating paramammal, *Lystrosaurus*, became semi-aquatic, living in the same kind of way that a hippopotamus does today, partly on land and partly in the water. Its remains have been found in South Africa, India and the Antarctic, providing strong evidence that the continents were in fact once joined together.

Some of the descendants of the earlier insect eaters also took to the water. One, *Proterosuchus*, lived in rivers and lakes in the southern parts of Pangea, in exactly the same environment as *Lystrosaurus*. *Proterosuchus* was a flesh eater, feeding on fish but also taking animals that came to the water's edge to drink, just as crocodiles do today. *Proterosuchus* and its relatives were the very first archosaurs and were the first true ancestors of the dinosaurs. Though at the beginning of the Triassic they must have been a minor danger to the paramammals, they did not seem to be any serious threat.

Two other groups of animals which must have seemed quite unimportant at the time were also to become dominant on land. One group, relatives of *Proterosuchus*, included a small, two-legged reptile called *Euparkeria*, which was an active hunter of other small reptiles and paramammals. The second group consisted of small, insect-eating animals rather like lizards. *Euparkeria's* descendants became the dinosaurs while the small insect eaters gave rise to the true lizards.

During the Triassic, reptiles gradually spread into many environments which until then they had ignored. Until the Triassic, for example, they had not colonized the warm, tropical waters of the ocean of Tethys, probably because there was ample food for them in the lakes and rivers of the land and little in the seas. However, many groups of bony fishes which had moved into fresh water during the Devonian nearly 200 million years before, now returned to the sea. The reptiles which fed on them followed. The ichthyosaurs or 'fish lizards' developed large tail fins to improve their swimming and lost the ability to move on land. They also stopped laying eggs and instead gave birth to live young. Gradually they became the dominant animals in the sea.

Other reptiles remained shore based. There were web-footed, fish-eating nothosaurs, paddle-finned plesiosaurs and a strange group called placodonts, with heavy, turtle-like shells. Some small, true lizards, the descendants of the insect eaters, also moved onto the shores.

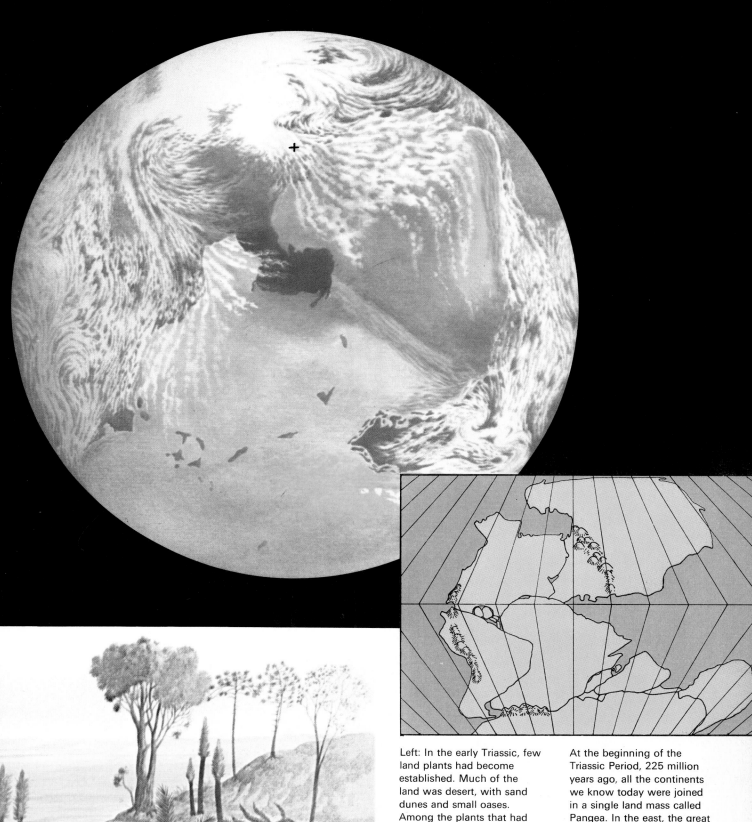

Left: In the early Triassic, few land plants had become established. Much of the land was desert, with sand dunes and small oases. Among the plants that had evolved were conifers and monkey puzzle trees, bamboo-like *Pelourdea*, cycads, ferns, horsetails and clubmosses.

At the beginning of the Triassic Period, 225 million years ago, all the continents we know today were joined in a single land mass called Pangea. In the east, the great Ocean of Tethys divided Pangea into two main sections, the northern, Laurasia, and the southern, Gondwanaland. Today, the Mediterranean Sea is all that remains of this vast ocean.

The shoreline provided a variety of environments in a small area. Cliffs and caves were safe refuges from enemies; there were all kinds of animals to be found stranded on the beach and used as food, while fishing in shallow waters for shellfish or crustaceans was another successful way of life. The lizards made good use of their new environments, though with the exception of one specialized fishing lizard, they did not colonize the sea itself.

Sea cliffs provided ideal conditions for the first experiments in flight and the first evidence of a flying vertebrate comes from Triassic rocks discovered on the edge of what was the ocean of Tethys.

The first flyers were probably shore-based vertebrates which, having clambered up the cliffs to escape danger, found it useful to be able to parachute down again when the threat had passed. There are always upcurrents of air along cliff faces and the animal's next evolutionary step would be to develop parachute membranes which would allow it to be carried upwards.

No observer of life in the early Triassic could have foreseen the complete reversal of the established order of the time. The semi-aquatic *Proterosuchus*, the tiny insect-eating lizards and the two-legged *Euparkeria* seemed quite insignificant; they

Proterosuchus

Lystrosaurus

could not possibly have looked like a threat to the paramammals, which had been the undisputed masters of the land for over 70 million years.

But though they continued to dominate the land during much of the Triassic, the paramammals made little attempt to find and use new environments. This was left to the reptiles, to the archosaurs in the rivers and lakes and to the small lizards on the shores of Tethys. They adapted to their new ways of life free from competition and as they adapted they became more efficient. When they later entered the territory of the paramammals, full of peaceful plant eaters, they soon established themselves as the dominant vertebrates.

Some lizards remained on the shores, others spread successfully over the uplands, but it was the return of the semi-aquatic archosaurs to dry land that finally sealed the fate of the paramammals. As fast-moving flesh eaters, their effect was devastating. Only the largest plant-eating paramammals and a few large flesh eaters survived until the end of the Triassic and by the beginning of the next Period, the Jurassic, only one vole-like creature was left. The smallest paramammals evolved into truc mammals and became largely nocturnal. The rest became extinct.

At the beginning of the Triassic Period, 225 million years ago, the paramammals were the most important reptiles on earth. In the swamps and rivers lived the plant eater *Lystrosaurus*, while on land the hairy *Cynognathus* and the small *Thrinaxodon* were fierce flesh eaters. Two other reptiles were also becoming important. *Proterosuchus* was a scavenging, semi-aquatic archosaur, the very beginning of the dinosaur line. *Prolacerta*, a small insect eater, was the ancestor of the lizards.

Cynognathus

Thrinaxodon

Prolacerta

THE ORIGIN OF DINOSAURS

The changes that led to the evolution of the first true dinosaur began many millions of years earlier, while the paramammals were still dominant. The ancestors of both the dinosaurs and of all modern reptiles were then small lizard-like animals, little more than 30 cm long, which slithered over the ground in search of insects. Their descendants developed into two major evolutionary lines, the true lizards, which at first continued to be insect eaters and the archosaurs, from which crocodiles, dinosaurs and birds evolved.

The first archosaur that is reasonably well known is *Proterosuchus* which, as we have seen, lived in freshwater lakes and rivers in the southern parts of Pangea. *Proterosuchus* was 1·5 m long, with a long head and a battery of powerful teeth, proving that it was a flesh eater. It still walked in a sprawling position on land, with the bones of its upper limbs held out sideways. *Proterosuchus* fed on fish and armoured amphibians and would certainly have sometimes taken *Lystrosaurus*, the paramammal that lived in the same rivers and lakes. Until *Proterosuchus* evolved, there were no other similar water-living predators, but from the dramatic way it developed we know that it had obviously found a successful way of life.

A descendant of *Proterosuchus* soon returned to dry land. This was a heavily-built animal with massive jaws and a short, squat body called *Erythrosuchus* when it was found in Africa and *Shansisuchus* in China. Such heavy creatures could have attacked the large plant-eating paramammals and may also have been general scavengers, but they were too slow and clumsy to do much harm.

The main evolution of the archosaurs during the early part of the Triassic took place in the rivers and lakes. One group that became very successful in India, Europe and North America was the phytosaurs. These lived in much the same way as crocodiles do today and at first glance they look just like modern crocodiles. They had the same pattern of bony scutes or plates beneath the skin, acting as an almost impenetrable armour, and the same ornament of small pits on the bones of the skull. The main outside difference was that the phytosaur's nostrils were close up in front of its eyes while the crocodile's are at the tip of its snout.

Phytosaurs, like crocodiles, were flesh eaters but there were also plant-eating archosaurs in the early Triassic lakes and rivers. The one we know most about is called *Stagonolepis*, from Scotland.

Holes in Triassic sandstones show where its bones were buried and from rubber impressions of these natural moulds the complete skeleton, with its bony armour, has been reconstructed. The descendants of *Stagonolepis*, such as *Typothorax* in North America and *Aetosaurus* in Germany, developed large, bony plates and spines to protect them from their more aggressive flesh-eating relatives.

Whether the water-living archosaurs were plant eaters or flesh eaters, they had certain basic features in common. All had some kind of bony armour and all developed a heavy, muscular tail. The sides of the tail became flattened so that it acted as a kind of paddle, driving the animal through the water as it moved from side to side. As the muscles grew more powerful, it became useful not only for swimming, but as a weapon and a means of defence.

A further development which helped the archosaurs to swim more efficiently was the increase in length and strength of the back legs. In the water, an animal needs back legs that are longer and stronger than its front legs, to give it thrusting power. However, it is no good making the back

Around 250 million years ago, the forerunners of the dinosaurs were small, insect-eating reptiles such as *Millerosaurus* and *Youngina*, which walked on land with a sprawling gait, holding their legs out sideways. By the beginning of the Triassic, 25 million years later, their descendants had taken to the water where their tails and back legs grew stronger to help them to swim.

Millerosaurus

Youngina

Proterosuchus

legs longer if they still grow out sideways from the body. To be effective, they must grow downwards, under the body, so that they can sweep back, pushing against the water.

Gradually the archosaurs' limbs changed, in much the same way that the first amphibians had changed before they ventured onto land 125 million years earlier. Like the amphibians, the reptiles found the new position of their limbs a great advantage on land as well as in the water. The earliest known crocodile (*Protosuchus*) from the Triassic of North America, had clearly begun to walk in this way, with its stride lengthened by moving the limbs from the shoulders and hips instead of mainly from the elbows and knees like the sprawlers.

Like the bony fins of fishes and the first shelled eggs, longer back legs and a different posture evolved to enable the archosaurs to live more successfully in their normal environments. But, also like the earlier evolutionary events, they made even more important changes possible. Because the archosaurs developed heavy, muscular tails, back legs that were longer than their front ones, held in a new way, they were able to use an entirely new method of walking on land. They found it difficult to run on all fours with any rhythm but they could now stand on their back legs alone, with the heavy tail acting as a counterbalance to the head and body. They could run using only the back legs, holding the front legs free off the ground. The stride was exceptionally long and the legs supported the body more effectively. The important point about this was that they were now able to move faster on land than any four-legged animal of the time.

While all these changes were taking place, the archosaurs lived safely in the water, where the paramammals did not interfere with them. Once perfected the new two-legged dinosaurs invaded the territory of the paramammals.

THE FIRST FLESH-EATING DINOSAURS

The immediate forerunner of the dinosaurs was *Euparkeria*, which appeared 225 million years ago at the beginning of the Triassic, rather later than *Proterosuchus*. *Euparkeria* was a small archosaur, 60 cm to 1 m long. It was descended from earlier semi-aquatic animals and so had a long tail and hind legs that were slightly longer than the front

Proterosuchus, the first archosaur, gave rise to *Shansisuchus*, a heavily-built land reptile. *Shansisuchus* on land and *Stagonolepis* and the phytosaurs in the water no longer sprawled along like their small ancestors but stood higher on their strong legs. Over the next 30 million years the archosaurs' limbs changed and the first crocodile, *Protosuchus*, walked in quite a new way, with its body held well off the ground. Before long the archosaurs were to develop the two-legged walk of the flesh-eating dinosaurs.

Shansisuchus

Stagonolepis

Protosuchus

Protosuchus

Phytosaur

ones. It it usually shown running on two legs, but when its skeleton is examined carefully, it is clear that though it could walk on two legs, it normally moved about on all fours.

Euparkeria lived at the same time and in the same place as the large, flesh-eating paramammal *Cynognathus*. A sudden burst of speed on its hind legs would have helped it to escape from such dangerous predators and, as it was a flesh eater itself, would also have helped it to surprise its own prey.

In the side of *Euparkeria's* snout there was a window-like opening, with sloping sides rather like the sides of a basin. All the archosaurs had this opening though crocodiles no longer have it today. No-one really knows what it was for. One suggestion was that it held the jaw muscles but it is not the usual shape and does not seem to be in the right position for this. The most likely explanation is that it held a large gland. Today, lizards have a similar opening between the nostril and the eyes, for a salt gland. This is a special organ for getting rid of excess salt and it is found today in reptiles and birds which live in areas where there is a lot of salt or very little water. We do not know whether archosaurs developed a similar gland because they

lived in similar conditions, but their skeletons have been found in Triassic sea deposits in Tunisia and Germany as well as in inland waters which were excessively salty.

In the Upper Triassic, 200 million years ago, a new reptile appeared. At first it was thought to be just a more advanced version of *Euparkeria* but now scientists agree that it was a true dinosaur. *Ornithosuchus* was 2 to 3 m long and was much more heavily built than *Euparkeria*. Its head was proportionately much larger, and it had a frightening array of sharp, stabbing teeth. The gland on the front of its head was enormously developed. The skull itself was very narrow at the front, almost like a sharp beak, but very deep, showing that it had enormous jaw muscles. Its back and sides were covered with bony plates and on the neck these grew into sharp spines, to protect this vulnerable area from attack.

Ornithosuchus is recognized as the ancestor of all the large, flesh-eating dinosaurs that developed in the Jurassic and Cretaceous Periods. During the later part of the Triassic it was itself the most formidable dinosaur living. At first its descendants simply increased in size. Gradually the bony armour disappeared and their skin grew scaly, like

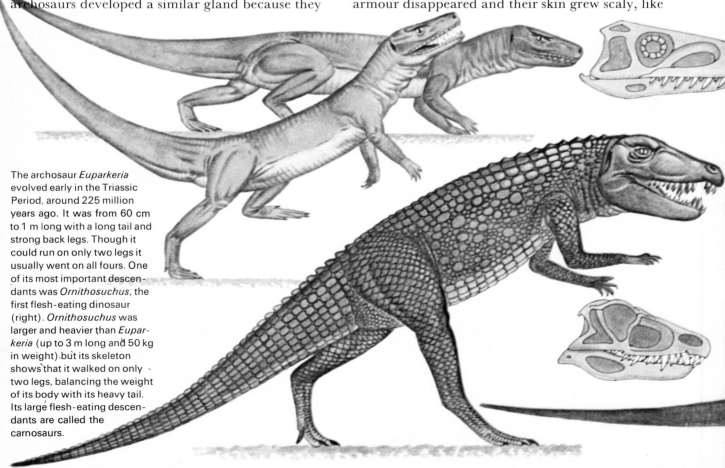

The archosaur *Euparkeria* evolved early in the Triassic Period, around 225 million years ago. It was from 60 cm to 1 m long with a long tail and strong back legs. Though it could run on only two legs it usually went on all fours. One of its most important descendants was *Ornithosuchus*, the first flesh-eating dinosaur (right). *Ornithosuchus* was larger and heavier than *Euparkeria* (up to 3 m long and 50 kg in weight) but its skeleton shows that it walked on only two legs, balancing the weight of its body with its heavy tail. Its large flesh-eating descendants are called the carnosaurs.

the skin of modern lizards. Since these dinosaurs had no real enemies, bony armour became unnecessary. The only danger to *Ornithosuchus* and its descendants would have come from other dinosaurs of their own kind, which would have attacked and eaten the younger, smaller animals.

Though all the large flesh-eating dinosaurs were descended from *Ornithosuchus*, another quite different group evolved, probably from a close relative of *Euparkeria*. The first of these, *Coelophysis*, from North America, is the same length as *Ornithosuchus* and, like it, was an active, two-legged flesh eater. But here the similarity ends. *Coelophysis* was extremely slender, weighing little more than 23 kg compared with the 50 kg *Ornithosuchus*. It had a long, slender neck and a small skull. Even its sharp, serrated teeth were tiny. Its tail was long, to balance the long neck and it had long, thin back legs. The first toe on the hind foot tended to point backwards like a bird's first claw, while the hands had long fingers that could well have been used for grasping prey. Throughout their history these small flesh eaters kept their long-fingered hands, while the arms of the larger, heavier flesh eaters grew gradually shorter and less effective.

The group of dinosaurs descended from *Ornithosuchus* are known as carnosaurs, while those descended from *Coelophysis* are called coelurosaurs. Though they were both flesh eaters, it is obvious that they could not have been in direct competition for food. The carnosaurs had massive skulls armed with dagger-like teeth and their powerful back legs had huge talons. Though they were dangerous animals, their great bulk must have reduced their speed and they had to rely on power and strength to overcome other slow-moving animals. The coelurosaurs were a complete contrast. They relied entirely on their agility to catch their prey. The long fingers of the hands could grab smaller animals or even rip at their flesh, while their long, flexible neck allowed them to reach out and snap their toothed jaws at insects, lizards or even recently-hatched dinosaurs. Because they were so different, carnosaurs and coelurosaurs were able to co-exist all through the Age of Dinosaurs as the only effective flesh eaters on the land.

Left: The skulls of *Euparkeria* and *Ornithosuchus* show their strong, stabbing flesh-eater's teeth and the basin-like hollow between eye and nostril which housed their special gland.

Their hip girdles, seen from the front, show the different positions of their upper leg bones. *Euparkeria*'s (left) projects sideways while *Ornithosuchus*'s grows down vertically under its body.

The other group of flesh-eating dinosaurs, the coelurosaurs, were descended from *Coelophysis*, which lived at the same time as *Ornithosuchus*. Its body was around 2 m long, the same size as *Ornithosuchus*, but it was much lighter and more agile, with a smaller head and a longer tail and neck. Carnosaurs and coelurosaurs were the very first dinosaurs to evolve and their direct descendants survived throughout the Age of Dinosaurs, for 140 million years.

THE FIRST PLANT-EATING DINOSAURS

In the Triassic rocks of North America and Europe, innumerable trackways of footprints have been known since the early days of the last century. The most famous were made by an animal which was named *Cheirotherium* – 'beast or mammal hand'. The name was given because the prints looked as if they had been made by a mammal's hand, with the first digit (the thumb and the big toe) separated from the others, exactly as they are in a human hand. In fact this 'thumb' was the fifth digit (equivalent to the little finger or toe) and was a characteristic of the early archosaurs like *Euparkeria*. *Cheirotherium's* feet were almost exactly the same as *Euparkeria's*.

When the footprints were first discovered, dinosaurs were completely unknown. People knew that they could not really have been made by a mammal and the general view was that they belonged to some kind of giant amphibian. A famous restoration was made of this supposed animal walking to make a line of footprints. There was one serious problem: the thumb and big toe were on the outside of the hand and foot, so the animal had to cross its legs at every step!

No-one has ever found any reptile bones near these footprints but in spite of this it is possible to work out what the animal really looked like. We know that there was a considerable difference in size between the back and front legs, for the prints of the feet are nearly twice as big as those of the hands. Though *Cheirotherium's* feet were like *Euparkeria's* the trackway is narrow, proving that unlike the sprawling *Euparkeria*, its limbs were held directly underneath its body. The body itself was held well clear of the ground, and as there are no tail tracks, we know that this did not drag along behind it.

The pattern of the foot- and handprints shows exactly how *Cheirotherium* walked, moving a front and back leg from opposite sides of the body in turn. When the left foot was forward, just behind the left hand, the right foot was in the rear position and the right hand was moving forward to make the front print. As the right foot moved forward behind the right hand, the left hand also moved forward to take the next step.

By measuring the distance between handprints, it is possible to work out where the shoulder joint was. The position of the hip joint can be worked out in the same way from the footprints and the distance between shoulder and hip can then be

The fossil footprint of *Cheirotherium* looks very like the imprint of a human hand. In fact the 'thumb' was the fifth digit, the little finger or toe, which stuck out sideways to give a firmer grip on the ground.

None of *Cheirotherium's* bones have ever been found but from the many trackways of footprints, scientists worked out exactly how it walked and what it must have looked like (bottom). Many years later a complete skeleton was found which looked just like the reconstructed *Cheirotherium*. The new skeleton (below) was named *Ticinosuchus* and was 2 to 3 m long. It was not a dinosaur itself but was the ancestor of a new group of plant-eating dinosaurs which were to become the largest land animals ever known.

found. This gives the scientist an accurate idea of the size of the animal's body.

Many years after the scientific restorations of *Cheirotherium* had been made, a complete skeleton of a very similar animal, *Ticinosuchus*, was found in the Tessin Alps in Switzerland. *Ticinosuchus'* feet still had the separated fifth digit, but its hands did not. This does not mean that it was not connected with *Cheirotherium*, simply that it was a more advanced land animal. The separated fifth digit helped to give the feet a firm grip on the ground and as the animal's walk improved, it became unnecessary. It moved back towards the other fingers and toes, became smaller and sometimes disappeared entirely.

There is, of course, no way to prove that the skeleton and the footprints belonged to the same animal, but there is no doubt that the four-footed *Ticinosuchus* and *Cheirotherium* were closely related.

Although *Ticinosuchus* was not itself a dinosaur, it became the ancestor of a new dinosaur sub-group which in turn was to give rise to the largest land animals ever known, the sauropods.

One of the early animals in this group was *Thecodontosaurus*. It was about the same size as its ancestor *Ticinosuchus* (2–3 m) but had a longer neck and a smaller head. Its teeth were still those of a flesh eater, but they were now small, serrated blades rather than stabbing points.

As a flesh eater *Thecodontosaurus* seems to have been in a difficult position. It could not have tackled prey as efficiently as *Ornithosuchus*, nor could it have defended itself successfully from other carnosaurs. On the other hand it was too bulky to dart about like *Coelophysis* and the coelurosaurs.

Thecodontosaurus was important for two reasons. First, it evolved – like all the other dinosaurs – from a four-legged reptile; but although it, too, could move on two legs, it was usually content to keep all four legs on the ground. Secondly, it heralded a change in dinosaur diet.

Since dinosaurs of all kinds were descended from flesh- or fish-eating reptiles, yet evolved into both plant- and flesh-eating forms, there must at some point have been a fundamental change from one type of food to another. *Thecodontosaurus* and its relatives mark just such an in-between stage, when a largely meat diet began to be mixed with plant foods. Before long, these forerunners of the great sauropods had changed to a wholly plant diet.

Thecodontosaurus (below, right) was the first dinosaur to start eating plants, though it still ate other reptiles as well. Its fossil skeleton, 2–3 m long, has been found in England and Germany.

Massospondylus (bottom), a close relative of *Thecodontosaurus*, was twice as long and was found thousands of kilometres away in southern Africa. Its teeth show that it, too, was becoming adapted to vegetarian foods.

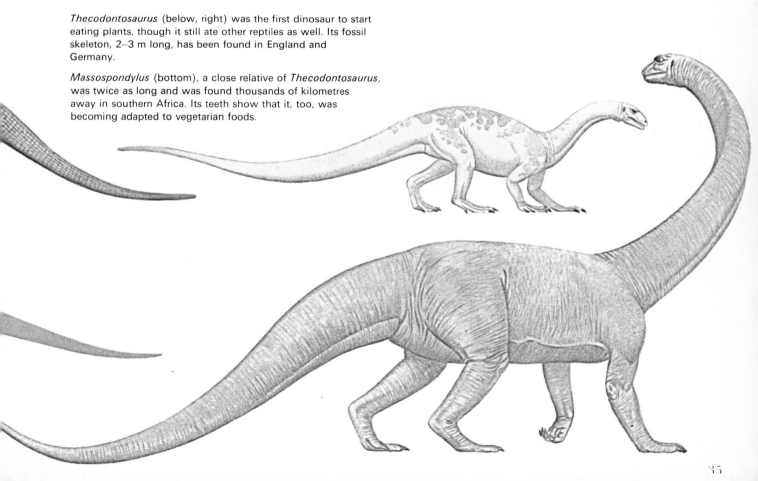

THE FIRST WARM-BLOODED DINOSAUR

Though later there were to be a great variety of different plant-eating dinosaurs, at the end of the Triassic there was only one large group of successful vegetarians. These forerunners of the great sauropods lived in Europe and Asia from England to China, in North America and in southern Africa.

While the plant-eating paramammals were dominant, the first efficient food chain had become established, with large numbers of plant eaters providing food for a few flesh eaters. When the first dinosaurs arrived, they not only destroyed the paramammals, they also destroyed the food chain, for they were at that time all flesh eaters.

It is hardly possible to populate the land entirely with flesh eaters. With only one another to feed on, they would soon die out. However, plants provide food in almost inexhaustible quantities and when plant-eating dinosaurs eventually evolved, the stable food chain was established once again. Most animals now fed on plants, in their turn providing food for the flesh-eating dinosaurs and for the scavengers that fed on the remains of their kills.

The best known of the early plant-eating dinosaurs is *Plateosaurus*. Like its ancestor *Ticinosuchus*, *Plateosaurus* walked on all fours. The fifth digit of the hand stuck out sideways like *Cheirotherium's*, proving that the hand must have been used for walking. We know from footprints that they often walked across soft, yielding sands and muds, where a broad hand was a great advantage. The thumb had a massive claw which could have been used for several things. It may have been a weapon against flesh-eating dinosaurs, it may have helped to hold the female during mating (several reptiles have claws or thumbs for this) or it may have given an extra grip on soft, muddy ground. The first and second fingers had smaller claws, and the last two none.

Though *Plateosaurus* normally walked on all fours, we know from some of the footprints that it sometimes ran on only its back legs. Its large tail balanced its head and body well, but being 6 m long, it would not have been able to run like this for very long. It probably used its two-legged run in short bursts, to escape from some danger. It would, however, have often stood on two legs. Many of the trees at this time had tall, bare trunks with bunches of fronds growing out of the top, rather like palm trees today. Standing on its back legs, with its long neck stretched out, *Plateosaurus* was 3 m tall and could easily reach the leaves.

Plateosaurus made another significant advance: it discovered that there was safety in numbers. Even though it was nearly twice as big as the flesh eaters of the time (the longest was 3 m long) it would be unlikely to come off well in a fight. But though a carnosaur could easily deal with a single animal, a herd was a different matter.

We know that *Plateosaurus* lived in herds because footprints show several animals of the same species all travelling in exactly the same direction. If these had been made by animals simply walking across the same area at different times, the trackways would not be parallel but would criss-cross.

Other evidence comes from groups of skeletons found lying together. We know from these that plateosaurs frequently died together, and it is safe to assume that they kept each other company while they were alive.

As well as living in a group, an animal can improve its chances of survival by growing larger. A vast bulk can in itself deter enemies and in nearly all types of plant eaters the animals gradually grow bigger as they evolve. As an animal grows larger, it takes longer to warm up or cool down. When it reaches a certain size the process is so slow that it is almost unnoticeable. The temperature inside the animal's body stays the same all the time and we say that it is warm blooded. *Plateosaurus*, twice the size of its ancestor *Ticinosuchus*, yet only a quarter as big as its giant descendants, was the first warm-blooded dinosaur.

Dinosaurs were not warm blooded in the same way that birds and mammals are. As we have seen, these keep their internal temperature steady by burning up their food quickly – a high metabolic rate – and insulating their bodies with fur and feathers while dinosaurs relied on their large size. Dinosaurs were simply too big to have a high metabolic rate. They would have had to burn up such vast quantities of food that they would have had to eat for more than 24 hours a day to keep going – and this is obviously an impossibility. Both types of warm-blooded animals must have a network of veins and arteries to carry the blood to the various parts of the body. With such a large bulk, the dinosaurs had to be particularly efficient at this and under the microscope it is possible to see a whole pattern of very fine blood vessels in a dinosaur bone. Their blood supply to the bone was in fact better than a man's.

Though dinosaurs did not need a high metabolic rate when they were fully grown, when they were young the situation was different. Even large dinosaurs were only a metre in length at hatching and would have had to grow at a great rate. If they had grown at the same speed as living reptiles, they would have been 200 years old before they reached their full, adult size! In fact we know from counting the growth rings on the bones of one full-sized dinosaur that it was 120 years old when it died. If an animal is to grow quickly, it must be warm blooded and as the young dinosaurs were not large enough to control their temperature by size alone, they may well have had a high metabolic rate. As they grew larger, the rate would have gradually slowed down, until when they were fully grown they had changed completely over to the other method.

Plant-eating dinosaurs evolved some time later than the flesh eaters, around 200 million years ago. One of the first was *Plateosaurus*, which is known from fossils found in England and Germany. *Plateosaurus* was 6 m long, twice as big as the flesh eaters of its time. Its back legs were much longer than its front ones but in spite of this it normally walked on all fours. When it ran on two legs or stood upright to feed on the tops of trees, its body and tail balanced each other perfectly over the hip region.

THE FIRST BIRD-HIPPED DINOSAURS

Towards the end of the Triassic Period, the largest of the forerunners of the sauropods lived in southern Africa. *Melanosaurus* was 12 m long, twice the size of its relative *Plateosaurus*. Size was obviously proving an advantage for although its smaller relatives became extinct, *Melanosaurus* became the first direct ancestor of the giant sauropods, one of the most successful of all dinosaur groups.

Really large dinosaurs, weighing 2 tonnes or more, could never have developed unless their limbs had already moved to stand like supporting columns under their great bodies. If they had still been sprawlers like *Euparkeria*, the tissues of the body wall would never have been able to bear the weight and the internal organs would have burst through. Because earlier animals such as *Ticinosuchus* had evolved an improved way of standing and walking, giant sauropods became possible.

While this group of dinosaurs was growing into larger and larger forms, another completely different kind was evolving. These were miniature dinosaurs, less than 1 m long, and were the earliest members of the second major division, the bird-hipped or ornithischian group.

Only one of these early bird-hipped dinosaurs, *Fabrosaurus*, is well known. *Fabrosaurus* was a plant eater, about 1 m long. It had long, slender back legs and much shorter front ones and was evidently a very good runner. It still probably walked on all fours when grazing along the ground, saving its two-legged run for short bursts of speed to escape from a flesh eater or chase a mate. Its feet were long and its hand still had the sideways fifth digit, but this was now quite small. All its other fingers had sharp claws.

Like all dinosaurs, the small bird-hipped species had to find a way of regulating their temperature so that they were neither too hot in the midday sun nor too cold at night. As we have seen, the large dinosaurs took so long to warm up or cool down that their internal temperature was almost unaffected by day and night changes, remaining roughly the same as the average daily temperature around them. The small dinosaurs were not big enough to be able to depend on size, and they did not have a high metabolic rate. Instead they used the same method of temperature control that some tropical lizards use today. When *Fabrosaurus* began to be too hot, it would seek the shade and when it began to get too cold, it would return to the sunlight. At night it would be in a state of torpor as

its body temperature fell, but because it was small, it would have warmed up again quickly in the first rays of the sun.

At first sight, *Fabrosaurus* looked very like the small two-legged flesh eaters of its time, the coelurosaurs. There were, however, two important differences. The first was in the way the three bones of the hip girdle were joined together. It is this difference that separates the dinosaurs into their two major groups, the lizard-hipped (saurischians) and the bird-hipped (ornithiscians).

The hip girdle consists of three main bones, the ilium, the pubis and the ischium. In the first group, the lizard-hips, the ilium is fixed onto the vertebrae, the pubis bone points forwards and the ischium backwards. The second group, the bird-hipped dinosaurs, have the same three bones. The ilium is still fixed to the vertebrae, and the ischium still points backwards, but the pubis bone has moved back so that it lies up against the underneath part of the ischium and has developed a new forward-pointing bone, called the prepubic process.

Ornithischians are called bird-hipped because their hip bones were arranged in exactly the same way as those of living birds. But do not be misled

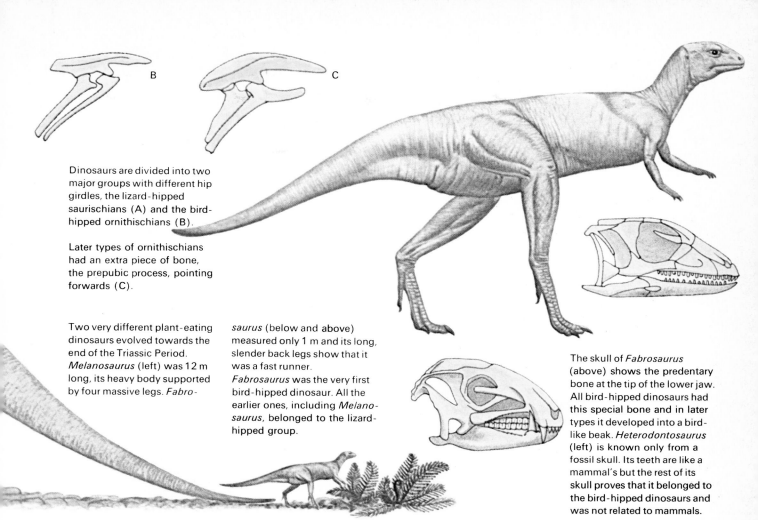

Dinosaurs are divided into two major groups with different hip girdles, the lizard-hipped saurischians (A) and the bird-hipped ornithischians (B).

Later types of ornithischians had an extra piece of bone, the prepubic process, pointing forwards (C).

Two very different plant-eating dinosaurs evolved towards the end of the Triassic Period. *Melanosaurus* (left) was 12 m long, its heavy body supported by four massive legs. *Fabro-saurus* (below and above) measured only 1 m and its long, slender back legs show that it was a fast runner. *Fabrosaurus* was the very first bird-hipped dinosaur. All the earlier ones, including *Melanosaurus*, belonged to the lizard-hipped group.

The skull of *Fabrosaurus* (above) shows the predentary bone at the tip of the lower jaw. All bird-hipped dinosaurs had this special bone and in later types it developed into a bird-like beak. *Heterodontosaurus* (left) is known only from a fossil skull. Its teeth are like a mammal's but the rest of its skull proves that it belonged to the bird-hipped dinosaurs and was not related to mammals.

into thinking that this means they were the ancestors of the birds. As we shall see later, the first bird was, in fact, descended from the lizard-hipped group, the coelurosaurs.

The second important difference between the saurischians and the ornithischians is in the bones of the skull. *Fabrosaurus* had small, sharp teeth which ground against one another, giving a good cutting edge for dealing with plants. At the front of its jaw, however, there was a wide gap where there were no teeth, but where a special bone, the predentary bone, grew. This bone, which was covered with a sharp horny beak for cutting leaves and twigs and tough plant material, is not found in any other group of reptile. It is the trademark of the ornithischian dinosaurs.

Heterodontosaurus, another small ornithischian dinosaur living at the same time as *Fabrosaurus*, is known only from a skull and a lower jaw. The shape of its skull, with the large opening for the gland, tells us that it was a dinosaur and its jaw, with the extra predentary bone, shows that it was an ornithischian. It is especially interesting because its teeth are much more like a mammal's than a reptile's. Though we know that it was not

connected in any way with either the later mammals or even the earlier paramammals, if the teeth alone had been found without the skull and jaw, everyone would have been sure that they belonged to a mammal. *Heterodontosaurus* helps to emphasize that dinosaurs developed an astonishing variety of different modifications to help them in their different ways of life.

From such forms as *Fabrosaurus*, there evolved a great number of plant-eating ornithischian dinosaurs which were to become far more varied than their saurischian relatives. Gradually more and more are being discovered, but there may be hundreds of others which have vanished for ever.

ANIMALS OF THE LOWLANDS

From studying the Triassic rocks of England, Germany and eastern North America, it is possible to tell what kind of world it was that the reptiles lived in 210 million years ago. Three main types of environment are known: the lowlands, the uplands and the shores of the great ocean of Tethys.

The lowlands were dry, semi-deserts with sand dunes and deep gullies gouged out by sudden downpours, rather like the wadis in modern deserts. Rivers flowed seasonally, draining into extensive inland lakes. In the waters lived armoured amphibians, bony fishes, crustaceans and shellfish and both in and around were abundant plants: ferns, horsetails, cycads and conifers.

When the lakes shrank in the dry season and the rivers were reduced to strings of isolated ponds, large tracts of bare sands and muds were exposed. In the heat of the sun the mud dried out. Cracks appeared and rain spots from the occasional light shower pitted the surface. As the wind drove the desert sands across the mud, the suncracks and even the rain prints were covered and preserved.

In many layers of these Triassic sands and muds, the surfaces are covered with footprints of all shapes and sizes. Here is evidence of abundant life on the move. In most cases it is possible to fit the footprints to the foot bones of known skeletons. The main groups of reptile living at the time can therefore be identified but the footprints show that there were more species in each group than there are skeletons preserved. They also show that some groups of reptile were living long before the time of the oldest known bones. The sets of footprints are especially valuable because we can see where animals were actually living: fossil skeletons show only where the dead bodies finally came to rest.

Herds of plant-eating dinosaurs grazed on the vegetation and sometimes entire groups were overwhelmed by sand storms or were caught in a flash flood after heavy rain, when tonnes of water rushed down the gullies sweeping all before it. The more massive of the flesh-eating dinosaurs, the carnosaurs, hunted food in the same regions. These two groups of dinosaurs were the heaviest reptiles of the time and their footprints are comparatively rare. This does not mean that there were fewer of them than of some other animals, simply that they did not walk across the mudflats in search of food.

The most familiar footprints belong to *Cheirotherium*, or 'mammal hand'. As *Cheirotherium* was a semi-aquatic flesh-eater and scavenger, it is not surprising that so many of its footprints are preserved on the edges of lakes and ponds. Their hand-like prints are so prominent that it is easy to overlook the many smaller, long-fingered prints that are found with them, followed by the marks of a tail being dragged along on the mud. These more delicate prints belonged to a group of lizards which ran along on their finger tips and probably fed on insects and small crustaceans.

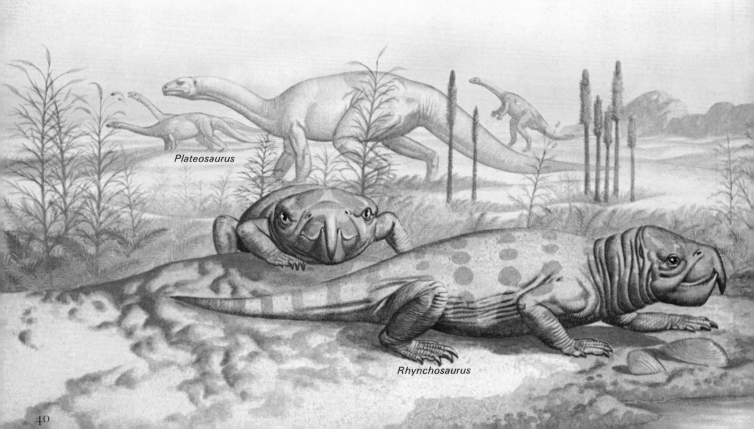

Plateosaurus

Rhynchosaurus

Some of the most unusual reptiles that evolved during the Triassic were the rhynchosaurs. These were compact, squat reptiles with powerful limbs. For a short period, in geological terms, they flourished and spread over most of the world. Their remains are found in Europe, India, East and South Africa, North and South America. They had a beak-like mouth with large, crushing teeth. Their jaws may have been used for cracking open the seeds of seed ferns, cycads and ginkgos, and the teeth were ideal for dealing with hard shells. Some people have suggested that they may have dug in the ground for roots, but more probably they ate molluscs such as freshwater mussels. Broken pieces of shell would have accumulated in the cheek pocket to be spat out later.

The other common reptiles of this time were the lightly-built, two-legged flesh eaters, the coelurosaurs. These hunted the small shore-living lizards and any other reptiles they could catch.

Finally, one further group of reptiles made its appearance at this time: the tortoises. *Proganochelys* the first tortoise, had a complete box-like carapace, and, unlike all its successors, it had teeth. The tortoises took to freshwater lakes and rivers and also later returned to the sea. Today some are flesh eaters, some plant eaters, and apart from losing their teeth, they have hardly changed throughout their long history.

ANIMALS OF THE UPLANDS

As we saw earlier, it is very rare for fossils from hilly regions of the earth to survive. There is little chance of the dead body of an animal being buried in sand or mud; it is much more likely to be worn quickly away by wind and rain. However, in the limestone hills of the Mendips and in South Wales, caves and cracks developed, leading deep into the earth. The bodies of animals that lived in these upland areas were often washed down and were preserved in the cave sediments.

The striking feature of the life found here is how modern it looks, with numbers of lizards and small mammals that would not be considered unusual there even today. The main flesh eaters were small dinosaurs and crocodiles but by far the most common animals were small lizards of various kinds.

The most dramatic of these was *Kuehneosaurus*, one of the earliest vertebrates to take to the air. *Kuehneosaurus* had long, hollow ribs that extended sideways to support a membrane of skin. It was similar to the flying lizard *Draco*, now found in the

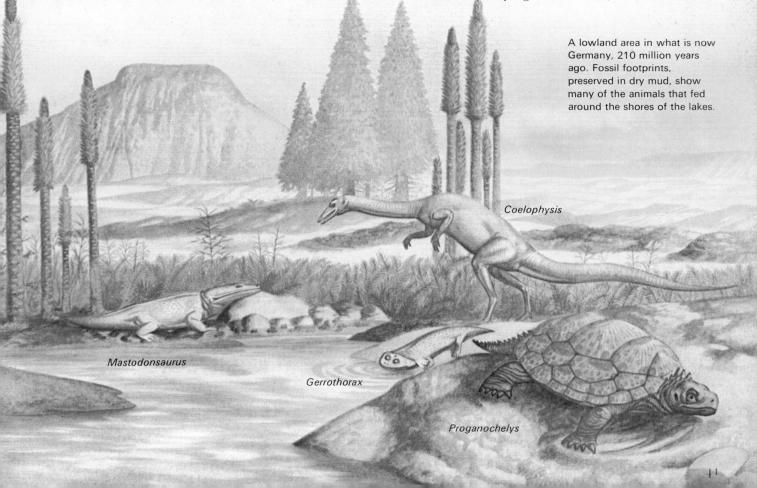

A lowland area in what is now Germany, 210 million years ago. Fossil footprints, preserved in dry mud, show many of the animals that fed around the shores of the lakes.

Coelophysis

Mastodonsaurus

Gerrothorax

Proganochelys

rainforests of Asia. Like *Draco*, it did not actually fly, but planed through the air from the tops of the trees: it was more of a parachutist than a glider.

Another common lizard was *Clevosaurus*, similar to the tuatara of New Zealand, which is now the sole survivor of this ancient group. These lizards have a characteristic downward turning snout and their teeth are fused to their jaw bones instead of fitting into sockets.

Two other reptiles are known from this area: procolophons, the larger ones, 1·30 m long, seem to have been the last descendants of the earliest reptiles. The others, the trilophosaurs, were small insect eaters, living in and around the rocky hill-sides. Their teeth had cusps for crushing insects.

In some places on the hills there were several early insect-eating mammals, which also ate some of the smaller lizards. The mammals were small, furry, shrew-like animals which were able to remain active during the night because they had a high metabolic rate.

Without the discovery of these unique cave

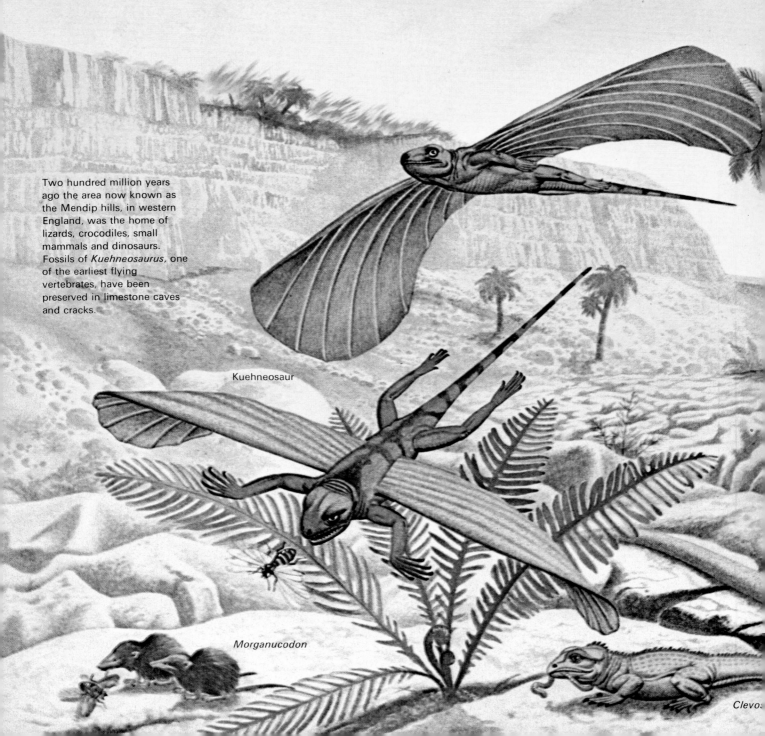

Two hundred million years ago the area now known as the Mendip hills, in western England, was the home of lizards, crocodiles, small mammals and dinosaurs. Fossils of *Kuehneosaurus*, one of the earliest flying vertebrates, have been preserved in limestone caves and cracks.

Kuehneosaur

Morganucodon

Clevos

deposits, the variety of animal life away from the open plains and swamps would have remained unknown, and we would have imagined quite a different scene.

THE SHORES OF TETHYS

Along the northern shores of the ancient ocean of Tethys were beaches, edged with cliffs and sea caves, where a large number of shore-dwelling animals were found. During the Middle Triassic, around 210 million years ago, sea water flooded a large area of land including much of what is now Germany.

A shallow, inland sea formed, joined to the ocean of Tethys by narrow straits in what is now south-west Poland. A string of islands made of black Devonian limestone stretched across the sea.

The best known of these ancient islands is known as the Isle of Gliny. Caves and cracks formed on its land surface, and on the shores there were sea caves. The beaches and cave floors were covered with rounded, limestone pebbles.

Large numbers of small animals lived on these beaches, finding their food either by scavenging at low tide or by swimming out to feed at sea. Occasionally *Ticinosuchus* would scavenge and hunt along the shores, but by far the most common reptiles were the fish-eating nothosaurs. These were basically true marine animals, but they were also able to move on land and the young sought refuge in the caves from the larger flesh eaters of the time. Even so, many died there and their worn bones, with those of the fish on which they fed, accumulated on the floor among the pebbles.

Yaleosaurus

Protorosaur

Trilophosaur

After the nothosaurs, the most common type of reptile were the lizards, which evolved here into many different shapes and sizes. One of the strangest was *Tanystropheus*. Though its body was proportioned like a normal lizard, its long neck sometimes measured as much as 3 m. The individual bones or vertebrae in this extraordinary, snake-like neck were longer than in any other animals, and some have been found that are 32 cm long, though only 1·5 cm thick. When these first bones were found, no-one connected them with *Tanystropheus*, which had been found earlier without a head or neck. It was not until many years later that a complete skeleton was found, with the long neck curled round the body.

It is difficult to understand what this incredible neck could have been for. Because each vertebra was so long, it could not have been very flexible, and it must have been very vulnerable to attacks from other reptiles. *Tanystropheus* was a flesh eater, probably feeding on small nothosaurs and fish. Perhaps its neck helped it to fish below the surface or to reach into rocky pools.

Other lizards that lived on the shores were less unusual. One, *Macrocnemus*, had a short, pointed snout and many sharp teeth: it was a scavenger and hunter of young nothosaurs. Another, *Askeptosaurus*, which evolved from *Macrocnemus*, became a sea-going fish eater. In fact it was the first real sea serpent, with a tail that grew into a long swimming organ.

Gliding lizards may also have lived on the Isle of Gliny, though at the moment the evidence is very slight: a single neck bone has been found in a Gliny cave, which is just like a bone from the neck of the upland gliding lizard *Kuehneosaurus*. News has recently been announced of the first pterosaur or flying reptile from the Triassic rocks of the northern shores of Tethys. The cliffs and rocks

The Isle of Gliny, now in south-west Poland. 210 million years ago most of this area was covered by a shallow, inland sea.

Tanystropheus

Ticinosuchus

Nothosaurus

Macrocnemus

44

would have made this coast an ideal place for small gliding or parachuting reptiles and though the very first fliers probably launched themselves from trees in the early Triassic uplands, perhaps it was here that the first lizards took to the air.

The cave deposits from the Isle of Gliny are the oldest ever known and as they contain an abundance of small animals not found anywhere else, they are especially important. The study of the fossils found there has been going on for many years. It is a very slow task, because every bone is separate: there is not a single complete skeleton. For each animal there will be many vertebrae, changing in shape and size from head to tail; different skull bones; bones from the shoulder and hip girdles; and all the individual bones from the front and back legs. All these, from many different animals are mixed up together. To make it even more difficult, some of the bones belong to reptiles that have never been found before. A few of the animals can be recognized easily because they have unmistakable characteristics – like the strange neck bones of *Tanystropheus*. Enough animals have now been identified to give us a good idea of the environment and the kind of animals living there, but there are still many discoveries to be made here.

Fossils of many different animals have been found in these cave deposits, including *Ticinosuchus*, *Macrocnemus* and the nothosaurs. One of the strangest lizards of all, *Tanystropheus*, hunted here, fishing with its 3 m long neck in the coastal waters.

Pterosaur

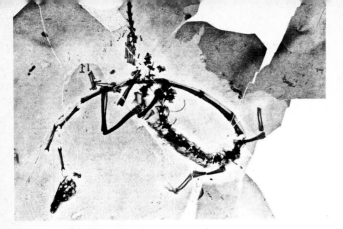

An X-ray photograph of the skeleton of *Tanystropheus* shows its enormously elongated neck attached to a normally proportioned head and body.

Below: Fossil skeleton of a nothosaur with its young. The rocks in which it was preserved were formed on the sea bed but have been lifted by earth movements and are now high in the Swiss Alps.

TRIASSIC MARINE REPTILES

Two other important events besides the rise of the dinosaurs took place during the Triassic period: the reptiles returned to colonize the sea, and they began to fly. Marine and flying reptiles were not dinosaurs, but in their own environments of sea and air they were just as important.

The most widespread of all the marine reptiles were the nothosaurs. They are found all over the shallow sea that spread across the flat plains of Europe, in England, Holland, Germany, France, Switzerland and Poland. If the northern shores of Tethys are followed as far as China and Japan, the nothosaurs are still there. On the southern shores they are found in Tunisia, Jordan and India.

Nothosaurs look very like most other primitive reptiles but in fact they were a completely independent group of animals. They are 30 cm to 6 m long, with tails flattened sideways for swimming, a

Askeptosaurus

Nothosaur

Mixosaurus

fin on their back and webbed feet. They had a long skull with many long, sharp teeth which prevented fish from slipping out of their mouth once they had been caught. We know that they could live on land because so many young ones have been found on the shores and in the caves, but they spent most of their lives hunting fish at sea.

Another group of reptiles of unknown origin also appeared in the Triassic – the ichthyosaurs or fish lizards. The first of these, called *Mixosaurus*, may have been descended from land-dwelling reptiles, but by the Triassic it had completely lost the ability to leave the water. *Mixosaurus* swam with its tail and had a tail fin like a fish, as well as a fin in the middle of its back. Its limbs had turned into paddles, rather like dolphins'. It gave birth to live young and did not lay shelled eggs on land.

The third group of marine reptiles were the placodonts, which were found all along the western shores of Tethys, from Jordan to Tunisia and to Germany and Switzerland. The placodonts were not related to any other group of reptile, though with their heavy bony carapace they look rather like long-tailed tortoises. Unlike tortoises, however, the armour was usually only well developed on the upper surface.

They had strong, crushing teeth which they used to crack the shells of crustaceans or shellfish. Some had pointed teeth for pulling the shells from the ocean bed, while others had a bony beak.

At the end of the Triassic the placodonts died out, and their place in the ocean was taken by the bony fishes – the same group from which the very first amphibians had evolved 150 million years before. These bony fish now developed powerful jaws and teeth and became much more efficient ocean dwellers than the placodonts. They breathed through gills, so did not have to come to the surface for air and they did not need to leave the water to lay their eggs.

Placodus (placodont)

Placochelys (placodont)

While dinosaurs were developing on land, other reptiles returned to the sea. In the Triassic nothosaurs were the most widespread marine reptiles. Others, such as ichthyosaurs like *Mixosaurus*, were to become dominant in the next Period, the Jurassic. Placodonts such as *Placodus* and *Placochelys* died out after the end of the Triassic. *Askeptosaurus*, with its sea-serpent-like tail was the only Triassic lizard to become fully marine.

FLYING AND PARACHUTING REPTILES

Sordes pilosus

At the beginning of the Triassic the reptiles first launched themselves into the air. The first fliers seem to have been small insect eaters belonging to the same group which gave rise to the dinosaurs. Some of these colonized the freshwater rivers and lakes, but others remained on land, taking refuge in the trees from the dominant paramammals.

Two remarkable parachuting reptiles were discovered in the 1970s near Osh in Soviet Kirgizstan, on the northern side of the Himalayas. They are particularly interesting because the fine details of their scales and skin are perfectly preserved and they provide important evidence of the way in which the two major groups of active flying vertebrates, the birds and the pterosaurs, could have originated. The other group of Triassic flying vertebrates, the gliding lizards or kuehneosaurs, were passive gliders or parachutists and they never developed into active fliers.

The two reptiles are called *Longisquama insignis* 'remarkable long scale', and *Podopteryx mirabilis*, 'marvellous foot wing'. *Longisquama* is important mainly for its scales, which represent the first stage in the evolution of feathers. The beginning of the bird's wing was developed along the back edge of the front limbs. Along the back there was a series of enormous scales that acted as a parachute and formed a frightening crest when the animal was at rest. In many ways *Longisquama* looks ideal as an ancestor of the birds, but in fact it became so good at gliding that it did not need to develop powered flight.

Podopteryx was the ancestor of the pterosaurs, the first flying reptiles to fly with a true, flapping flight. *Podopteryx* itself was a glider. Its gliding membrane or parachute was made from skin stretched between its tail and its back legs. Another membrane of skin grew from each side of its body, joining the knee of each back leg to the elbow of each front one.

The membrane skin was elastic and was controlled mainly by the back legs. As pterosaurs evolved, their front membranes grew larger, until they stretched to the ankle of the back legs and became attached to a long fourth finger on the front hand. By the time this happened, pterosaurs had become active, powered fliers and they controlled both lift and forward movement by the front instead of the back membrane. With their large, leathery, wings flapping slowly through the air they must have looked like modern fruit bats

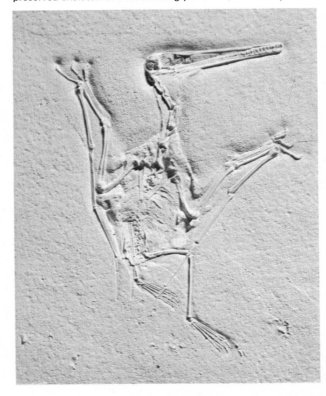

Pterosaurs probably evolved during the Triassic Period. Above: Thick fur on the leg of *Sordes pilosus*. Below: Perfectly preserved skeleton of a 22 cm long pterosaur, *Pterodactylus*.

Podopteryx mirabilis

Longisquama insignis

Pterodactylus

At the beginning of the Triassic Period, the archosaurs took to the air. *Podopteryx* developed a skin membrane for parachuting and gliding and eventually its descendants evolved into true, flying pterosaurs (far left). *Longisquama* grew long, overlapping scales which in time became feathers. They enabled it to glide from trees and when it was at rest formed a large crest over its back.

Below: The stages of a pterosaur's flying movement. Pterosaurs flew in basically the same way as birds but they controlled the curve of their wings with their back legs. On the downstroke, which drove them through the air, they stretched their legs and arms to make all the membranes as wide as possible. On the upstroke the wing was folded to reduce wind resistance.

flying – as Alice in Wonderland said, 'like a tea tray in the sky'.

The first complete pterosaur skeleton is around 190 million years old and comes from the Lower Jurassic rocks of southern England. Parts of pterosaur fossils are also known from earlier times. This first skeleton, *Dimorphodon*, had a large head and a long, bony tail. In 1971, however, a complete pterosaur, not just a skeleton, was discovered in Upper Jurassic rocks near Chimkent in Soviet Kazakhstan. It was called *Sordes pilosus*, or 'hairy filth' and it answered many of the questions that had puzzled scientists.

The flying membrane was perfectly preserved, and it was easy to see that the membrane between the back legs was no longer attached to the tail. But the most sensational aspect of *Sordes pilosus* was the fact that it was covered in thick fur. The fur was thickest around the thigh, but stretched right down the legs to the ankles. There was even fur on the underneath of the wing membrane, between the knee and the elbow and between the back legs. There was also a patch of fur on the inside of the elbow. The actual body had a thick, furry coat which has been amazingly preserved in the rock.

Because of this discovery, we can now say definitely that pterosaurs were not reptiles, as everyone had supposed. They were warm-blooded, furry fliers belonging to a completely different group of vertebrates. Though they have now disappeared, in their time they equalled the birds.

As pterosaurs became more expert fliers, further changes took place. They lost their teeth and tails. A long, stiff tail is useful for simple gliding but in proper flying it makes manoeuvring very difficult and adds extra weight. We know from pterosaur skeletons that many different kinds evolved. Some were long distance soarers, with long, narrow wings which acted like those of an albatross today; others had shorter, broader wings and could fly fast and actively.

The pterosaurs had eyes, brains and air-filled bones just like the modern birds but they were not directly related to them. The birds are not the descendants of the pterosaurs; they evolved the ability to fly quite independently.

The Jurassic Period – 190 to 136 million years ago

The Jurassic Period was a time of stability. The climate was wetter and warmer, so that although the plant life was not basically different from Triassic plant life, conifers and cycads now began to be more widespread and the maidenhair tree, the ginkgo, became common. Along river banks ferns and horsetails grew thickly.

Although we think of the Jurassic as a time of little change, it was during this Period that the supercontinent of Pangea began to break up into the continents we know today. This in turn led to different animals developing in different ways on the various land masses.

During the Jurassic all the major groups of reptiles that were to dominate the earth for the next hundred million years became firmly established. On the other hand, many of the reptiles which had evolved during the Triassic were not successful and now disappeared. In the seas, the mollusc-eating placodonts, the fish-eating nothosaurs that had been so widespread and the lizard *Askeptosaurus* all became extinct. On land the mollusc-eating rhynchosaurs vanished; many of the plant-eating reptiles and the crocodile-like phytosaurs disappeared from freshwater rivers and lakes. The armoured amphibians that had been common earlier in the Triassic were no longer found and gliders such as *Kuehneosaurus*, *Longisquama* and *Podopteryx* were no longer to be seen parachuting from the trees.

New, more efficient animals moved into the places now left empty. In the seas, sharks and rays flourished. The bony fishes developed jaws and teeth for eating shellfish, taking the place of the placodonts. The dolphin-like ichthyosaurs which had begun to evolve at the end of the Triassic became dominant, replacing the nothosaurs. Plesiosaurs, relatives of the extinct nothosaurs, also became important in the sea. Towards the end of the Jurassic the crocodiles, which had replaced phytosaurs as the main semi-aquatic flesh eaters, also returned to the ocean.

On land the dinosaurs were supreme. At the top of the food chain were the theropods, large and small flesh eaters from the saurischian or lizard-hipped group. They were active hunters of the large plant-eating sauropods, the other division of lizard-hipped dinosaurs, which lived in lowlands and swamps in the same regions.

Throughout the Jurassic, the lizard-hipped dinosaurs were dominant. The bird-hipped group – the ornithischians – which had appeared at the end of the Triassic with the lightly-built *Fabrosaurus*, were only a small part of the dinosaur scene. However, one large bird-hipped dinosaur *Camptosaurus* and a few armoured ones evolved in this period. They were the forerunners of the spectacular varieties that were to follow in the Cretaceous.

The dinosaurs on land and in the swamps, ichthyosaurs and plesiosaurs in the seas and pterosaurs in the sky formed the pattern of life in the Jurassic. But this was not the whole of the story. During this Period, 150 million years ago, the first bird, *Archaeopteryx* appeared. Turtles and tortoises became firmly established. The little lizards whose fingertip footprints were found all over the Triassic lowlands did not change, but there were important developments in other lizard groups. Before the Jurassic ended, 136 million years ago, most modern lizards – iguanas, geckos, skinks, lacertilians, even limbless slow-worms – were all there.

Finally, several new groups of mammals evolved, some small rodent-like plant eaters and several groups of insect eaters.

Birds, lizards and mammals were insignificant animals compared with the great reptiles of the Jurassic but, looking back, their establishment was probably the most significant event of the whole Age of Dinosaurs.

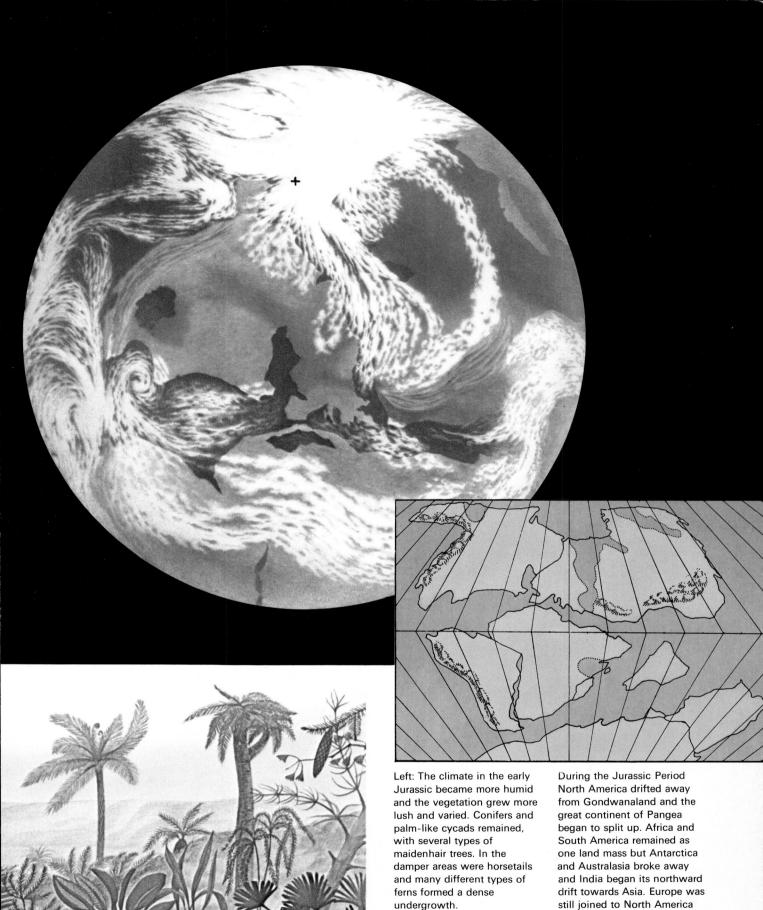

Left: The climate in the early Jurassic became more humid and the vegetation grew more lush and varied. Conifers and palm-like cycads remained, with several types of maidenhair trees. In the damper areas were horsetails and many different types of ferns formed a dense undergrowth.

During the Jurassic Period North America drifted away from Gondwanaland and the great continent of Pangea began to split up. Africa and South America remained as one land mass but Antarctica and Australasia broke away and India began its northward drift towards Asia. Europe was still joined to North America but was now separated from Asia by a shallow sea.

FLESH-EATING DINOSAURS

All the large, flesh-eating dinosaurs of the Jurassic Period were descended from the Triassic dinosaur *Ornithosuchus*. During the Jurassic, large numbers of giant plant-eating dinosaurs developed and appropriately-sized flesh-eating dinosaurs evolved to deal with each one.

The first dinosaur bone ever found belonged to *Megalosaurus* or 'giant lizard', and was described by Dr Robert Plot in 1677 in his book *The Natural History of Oxfordshire*. No-one knew what it was and Dr Plot suggested it was from a giant man. It was later named *Scrotum humanum* because it looked like a man's petrified scrotum.

In 1822, James Parkinson published a picture of a large tooth belonging to the same animal and named it *Megalosaurus*. *Megalosaurus* was a large flesh eater, really a magnified version of its ancestor *Ornithosuchus*. Up to 9 m long, it stalked in search of its prey on massive muscular hind legs. The shorter front legs had three powerful, clawed fingers.

One of the largest flesh-eaters of the time was *Allosaurus*. It was about 11 m long, as long as a motor coach and its three-toed feet ended in terrible, clawed talons. With such formidable weapons, it would kill its victims and would then tear out the entrails and flesh with its hands and its sharp, blade-like teeth. As it weighed 2 tonnes, it obviously could not move as fast as some of the smaller plant eaters. However, most of the main plant-eating dinosaurs were even heavier than *Allosaurus*, some as much as forty times its weight, so they had little chance of running away. *Allosaurus* was an active hunter and footprints have been found which show it following sauropods across the mud of a lagoon, taking strides 2 m long.

A close relative, *Ceratosaurus*, was only half the size of *Allosaurus*. Like *Allosaurus*, it had bony thickenings just above the eyes to protect it as it fought with its prey or with other flesh eaters, and it also had a bony spike on the tip of its snout. *Ceratosaurus* and *Allosaurus* were beautifully balanced, their long stiff, muscular tails sticking out behind as they bent over to feast on the body of a plant eater. *Allosaurus* would have lashed out with its tail to keep off other hungry dinosaurs; when it had eaten its fill it would have waddled off, to lie down to digest its meal. Even a large flesh eater is unlikely to have stayed sleeping by its kill; if it had, it would soon have been attacked.

During such a feast, a number of smaller dino-

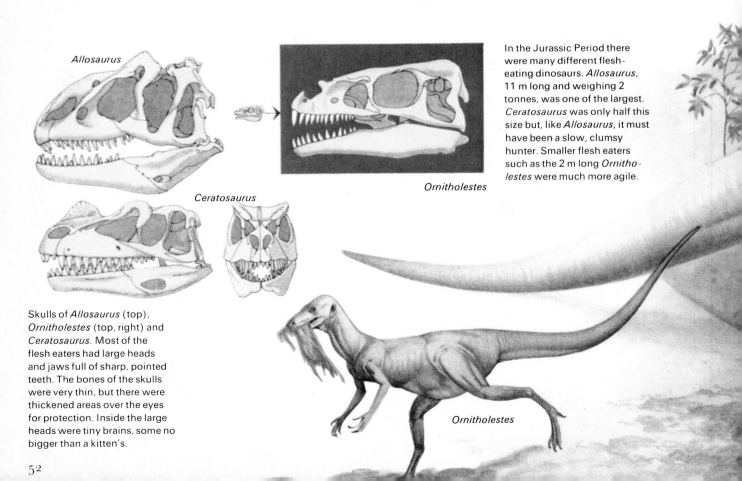

Allosaurus

Ceratosaurus

Ornitholestes

In the Jurassic Period there were many different flesh-eating dinosaurs. *Allosaurus*, 11 m long and weighing 2 tonnes, was one of the largest. *Ceratosaurus* was only half this size but, like *Allosaurus*, it must have been a slow, clumsy hunter. Smaller flesh eaters such as the 2 m long *Ornitholestes* were much more agile.

Skulls of *Allosaurus* (top), *Ornitholestes* (top, right) and *Ceratosaurus*. Most of the flesh eaters had large heads and jaws full of sharp, pointed teeth. The bones of the skulls were very thin, but there were thickened areas over the eyes for protection. Inside the large heads were tiny brains, some no bigger than a kitten's.

Ornitholestes

saurs, only 2 m long, would have arrived and darted in to snatch away choice pieces of meat. One of these was *Ornitholestes*, which had long, thin legs and a very long, stiff tail. Its hands had long, slender fingers which helped it to grab lumps of flesh and entrails. *Ornitholestes* was a descendant of the lightly-built Triassic coelurosaurs. Like them it was an active hunter and ate small reptiles and the young of the larger dinosaurs. It snapped up any mammal, even a grounded pterosaur, that it happened to disturb in the undergrowth.

The large flesh eaters were not agile enough to rummage in the thick bushes where smaller animals found a safe refuge. The coelurosaurs had no such difficulties and they were the main hunters of the more densely wooded regions. They also acted as general scavengers, tidying up the edible remains of the big kills, just as hyaenas and jackals do today after lions have finished with their prey.

The smallest dinosaur so far found is *Compsognathus*. It was a close relative of *Ornitholestes* but was only 30 cm long when fully grown. This tiny flesh eater, no bigger than a hen, could never have been of any danger to other dinosaurs, though it could perhaps have tackled their newly-hatched young. Mammals, small lizards and pterosaurs and insects must have been its staple food. One of the main problems that small dinosaurs like this faced was that the animals they hunted could escape by running up into a tree. The only way to be certain of a meal was to climb after them and it is very likely that this is just what *Compsognathus* did. It was a development that was to have very important consequences.

Ceratosaurus

Allosaurus

THE FIRST BIRD

The small, flesh-eating coelurosaurs such as *Compsognathus* do not seem very important among the dinosaurs, yet from them developed some of the most successful groups of all backboned animals, the flying and feathered birds.

Perhaps the most famous fossils ever found are those of the first bird, *Archaeopteryx* or 'ancient wing'. *Archaeopteryx* was like a tiny dinosaur covered in feathers instead of scales. Indeed, if it had been found without feather impressions it would have been considered simply as a special kind of dinosaur. Its first toe pointed backwards, allowing it to perch securely in trees, but otherwise it was very like the other dinosaurs. It had teeth and a long, bony tail; it had 'hands' with three long fingers and sharp claws. The only bird-like feature in its skeleton, apart from its backward pointing toe, was one of the bones of its hip girdle, the pubis. This pointed backwards like a bird's, not forwards like a coelurosaur's. But only the outline of *Archaeopteryx*'s feathers proved that it was really a true bird, not some new kind of flesh-eating, bird-hipped dinosaur.

Archaeopteryx had exactly the same number of feathers on its front limbs as modern birds have on their wings: 10 primary feathers and 14 secondary feathers. Because of this, it is universally accepted as the ancestor of all birds. Most scientists also now agree that *Archaeopteryx* is a direct descendant of the coelurosaurs. Two important questions remain.

Why did *Archaeopteryx* evolve feathers and why did it take to the air?

The questions are connected and there are two possible answers. First the ancestor of *Archaeopteryx* may, as a ground dweller, have developed feathery scales to help it to swoop onto its prey, covering it with a feathery canopy as the secretary bird does today. At the same time feathery scales would have helped it to make longer jumps and leaps as it ran, until eventually a leap would have launched it into the air.

The second, more generally accepted theory, is that *Archaeopteryx* climbed trees and that the feathers helped it to parachute down again like the early glider *Longisquama*.

Archaeopteryx was very active. It lived in densely wooded areas and its feathers played a very important role. They provided insulation, enabling it to keep its internal body temperature high and so remain active even when the outside temperature fell.

Though it had wings and feathers like a modern bird, *Archaeopteryx* could not really fly. Modern birds have massive breast muscles and air spaces within their bones for lightness. *Archaeopteryx* did not have the large muscles, but it had air-filled bones. It could plane down from the trees and could flap its wings to help it glide further; it could even twist and turn a little, but that was all. Its long, bony tail was useful in gliding, for it acted as an automatic stabilizer but its additional weight made long flights difficult and prevented *Archaeopteryx*

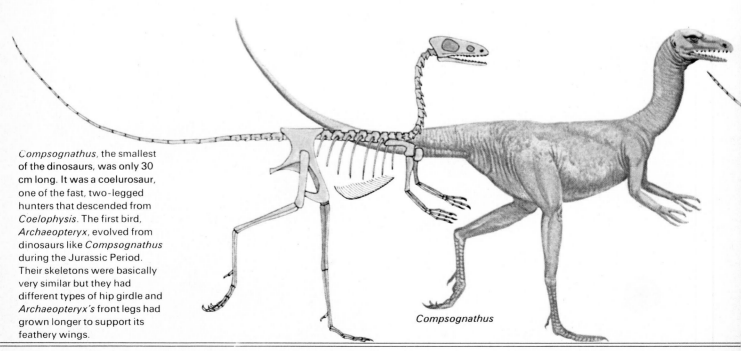

Compsognathus, the smallest of the dinosaurs, was only 30 cm long. It was a coelurosaur, one of the fast, two-legged hunters that descended from *Coelophysis*. The first bird, *Archaeopteryx*, evolved from dinosaurs like *Compsognathus* during the Jurassic Period. Their skeletons were basically very similar but they had different types of hip girdle and *Archaeopteryx*'s front legs had grown longer to support its feathery wings.

Compsognathus

from launching itself into the air from the ground.

At this time the air was dominated by the warm-blooded downy or furry pterosaurs. The pterosaurs were efficient fliers and because of this it may seem strange that the birds became established while pterosaurs disappeared completely. *Archaeopteryx* did not compete directly with the pterosaurs. It only survived because it lived in areas where pterosaurs could not go. The deep bushes were too dangerous for them, for once their delicate flying membranes were torn, they were doomed. In contrast, the feathers of the bird parted when they met any obstruction and even if they were torn, they would grow again. In this way the birds were able to evolve in isolation, free from pterosaur competition, until they had lost their teeth and tails and had acquired air spaces in their bones. Once they had become active, powered, flapping fliers, they could enter the territory of the dominant pterosaurs on equal terms.

When they reached this stage, the birds had one advantage which led to their ultimate success: a bird on the ground is as much at home as it is in the air. Its wing tucks into the side of its body and it can run about just like a miniature two-legged dinosaur. When a pterosaur was grounded it was in a very different state. It was slow and clumsy. Its wings tangled up with its back legs and it had to crawl along on all fours, an obvious target for predators. The birds which have evolved from *Archaeopteryx* are true dual-purpose animals, successful both on land and in the air.

Archaeopteryx had backward-pointing claws on its feet. When it perched on a branch, with its wings folded, the claws gripped like thumbs and held it securely. When its wings were spread, the claws on the front 'legs' helped it to climb and cling to the trunks of trees.

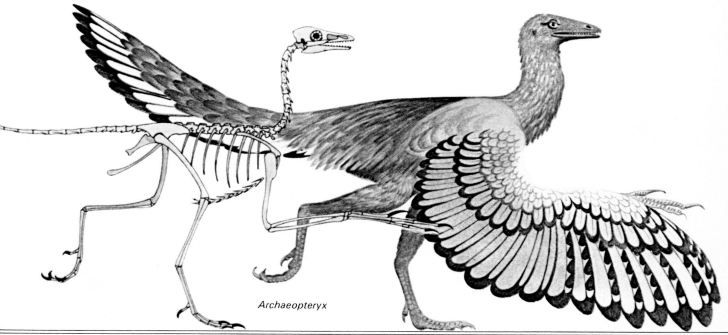

Archaeopteryx

THE GREAT SAUROPODS

The most sensational-looking of all the dinosaurs were the sauropods, giant plant-eating animals which evolved at the end of the Triassic Period, 190 million years ago. The two best known are *Diplodocus* and *Apatosaurus*, which used to be called *Brontosaurus*.

Diplodocus was one of the longest land animals that has ever lived. It was some 28 m from head to tail and weighed 10 tonnes. Most of its length was made up of its 14 m whip-like tail and its 8 m long neck. Its head was minute, with a brain only the size of a kitten's. Its deep, narrow body was held up by four massive pillar-like legs. Standing on all fours, with its neck and tail stretched out, *Diplodocus* was more than six times the length of a large rhinoceros.

Diplodocus' backbone was very light, for each bone was hollowed out. There may also have been air spaces within the bones to make them lighter still. Its small head and brain weighed very little. Though the bones of its body were light, *Diplodocus* was still a very bulky animal and to support its great weight, its legs were made of solid bone instead of being hollow cylinders like those of other vertebrates.

Each back foot had five toes, with horny claws on the first three. The outer two toes were enclosed in a huge, tough footpad, rather like the pad on an elephant's foot. The front feet had only a single claw, on the thumb, which acted as a hook to prevent the heavy dinosaur from slipping in the mud and was also used to hold the female during mating. On land they walked slowly and carefully,

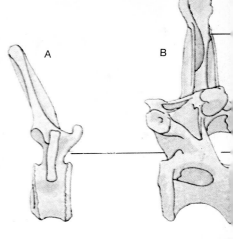

The giant plant eater *Diplodocus* was 28 m long – longer than a railway carriage – and weighed 10 tonnes. Its leg bones were solid pillars but the bones in its back were light and probably had air spaces inside them. In the tail, which hung down in the water, the vertebrae were solid (A). In the middle of the back they were hollow but had strong walls (B) and in the neck, which floated on the surface, they were light and delicate (C).

and they probably spent most of their time wading in the swamps, feeding on the soft vegetation.

Diplodocus was by no means the heaviest of the sauropods. *Apatosaurus*, though slightly shorter (25 m long), weighed over 30 tonnes, five times as much as a modern elephant. We know that these enormous creatures could walk on land, because they came ashore to lay their eggs, but they, too, spent most of their time in the swamps. The hollowed-out backbone helped to buoy the body up and the heavy legs helped to keep their feet on the bottom. Nostrils on the very top of their head enabled them to breathe when they were under water.

Many footprints are known which show that they moved about in groups with the adults on the outside and the young inside for protection, just as herds of antelopes or elephants do today. Sometimes the herd would travel across sand but generally they waded in mud at the bottom of the swamps.

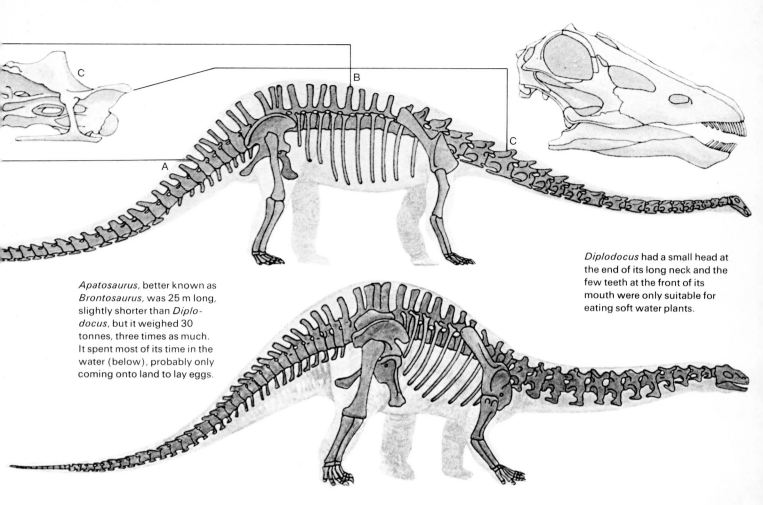

Apatosaurus, better known as *Brontosaurus*, was 25 m long, slightly shorter than *Diplodocus*, but it weighed 30 tonnes, three times as much. It spent most of its time in the water (below), probably only coming onto land to lay eggs.

Diplodocus had a small head at the end of its long neck and the few teeth at the front of its mouth were only suitable for eating soft water plants.

Footprints prove that they were able to float on the surface, their back legs kicking the water, and the tip of their long tail drooping down to the bottom as a kind of anchor. Only the front legs touched the bottom as they pawed their way along in the same way that hippopotamuses do today in the rivers of Africa. There is one famous set of footprints made by the front feet alone which shows exactly this. One back foot touched the bottom only occasionally when the animal made a turn.

Another group of sauropods had front legs that were longer than their back ones. They still walked solidly on four legs, but as their shoulders were higher than their hips, their great backs sloped

downwards from neck to tail, making them look rather like outsize giraffes. In other ways they were similar to the rest of the sauropods: their backbones were hollowed out and their skulls were extremely delicate, with tiny brains and a large nostril on the topmost part of the head.

The ancestor of this group, *Camarasaurus*, was 18 m long, quite short for a sauropod. Skeletons of young have been found which show that when they were only 5 m long they had comparatively large heads and short necks. As they grew older the proportions gradually changed to the typical adult form with a tiny head at the end of a long, muscular neck.

The largest of this group of sauropods was the towering *Brachiosaurus* which has been found in East Africa and North America. A mounted skeleton in the museum in Berlin is 23 m long, its head reaching up 12 metres, higher than a two-storey house. A fully-grown man does not even reach up to its elbow. It has been calculated that *Brachiosaurus* weighed 81 tonnes, eight times as much as *Diplodocus*. Recently an even larger skeleton has been found in America. This was over 30 m long and must have weighed over 100 tonnes, almost twice as much as a Chieftain tank.

Brachiosaurus was the largest land-going animal ever known, though like the other sauropods it spent most of its time in the swamps, breathing through the nostril at the top of its head when it was feeding under water. Its great bulk was certainly more manoeuvrable in the water than on land. Some people show *Brachiosaurus* walking on the river bed with its head just breaking the surface. In fact the lightness of the upper part of its body, the air spaces round its backbone and its air-filled lungs made it very difficult for *Brachiosaurus* to stay on the bottom, in spite of its heavy legs. But the real reason why it could not live so deep down was the tremendous pressure of water that would have been put on its lungs and on the blood vessels in its neck.

To submerge completely *Brachiosaurus* needed water at least 12 m deep. The water pressure at this depth would have crushed its lungs and constricted the veins and arteries of the neck so that blood would not have been able to reach the brain.

Like the other sauropods, *Brachiosaurus* let its long neck float at the surface of the water and rarely went out of its depth. Its long, strong fore-limbs helped it to clamber out onto the river banks and out of deep mud at the edge of the swamps.

The purely mechanical problems of carrying such an enormous weight must have been tremendous though its size probably made it safe from attack by flesh eaters. It probably lived further out in the swamps than the shorter legged sauropods like *Diplodocus*, so that it would not compete with them for food. Its enormous bulk required immense amounts of food to sustain it. Only the softest and mushiest kind was suitable, and this had to be taken in at a fast rate, as there was no time to chew tough plants. *Brachiosaurus* must have spent most of its time eating.

Up to a point, size gave the sauropods many advantages but *Brachiosaurus* may eventually have grown too big to survive. At any rate, very few of these giant sauropods lasted long into the next Period, the Cretaceous, when other groups of dinosaurs were at the peak of their success.

Some sauropods, however, survived right to the very end of the Age of Dinosaurs, for over 120 million years. They were completely unprotected by horns or bony armour and though they could perhaps have used their tails to lash out at an enemy, the real secret of their survival was that they lived out in the waters of the swamps where the flesh eaters did not venture.

Brachiosaurus, the largest land-going animal ever known, grew to 30 m long and weighed a massive 100 tonnes. Its high shoulders and long neck raised its head 12 m from the ground. It had a delicate-boned skull (left) with a jutting snout. Its nostrils were on a ridge at the top of its head so that it could breathe when the rest of its head was under water. Like the other sauropods it spent most of its time in the swamps, swimming and wading among the water plants.

Camarasaurus was a close relative of *Brachiosaurus* but it had shorter front legs and a shorter neck. Like *Brachiosaurus* it had a very delicate skull but its rounded snout makes its head look very different.

Below: Fossils of young dinosaurs are very rare but an almost perfect skeleton of a young *Camarasaurus* was found in Utah in 1922. This reconstruction shows clearly that when they were small, sauropods had quite short necks and large heads.

CAMPTOSAURUS

Among the successful animals of the Jurassic was a group of dinosaurs called the ornithopods. From a distance they might have been mistaken for two-legged flesh eaters like *Allosaurus* because they walked on only their back legs. From close by it would be possible to see that they were plant eaters, grazing and browsing on leaves from trees and bushes, and that instead of the frightening-looking talons of the flesh eaters, they had small hooves on their three-toed feet.

These dinosaurs moved about in large herds over the flat plains. They were larger than the flesh eaters of the time and though a single animal was defenceless and helpless, no flesh eater would have approached the entire herd.

These two-legged dinosaurs were descended from the small Triassic *Fabrosaurus* and belonged to the bird-hipped group. The larger forms such as *Camptosaurus* were the main evolutionary line, but several other types also developed. *Camptosaurus* was nearly 5 m long and weighed 3·7 tonnes: it was almost five times the size of its small ancestor *Fabrosaurus*. Its head was long and rather flat, con-

trasting with the short heads of the flesh eaters. Its ridged, closely-packed teeth were also very different from flesh eaters' teeth, for they were specially adapted for crushing and chopping up plant materials. Like *Fabrosaurus*, it had a sharp, bony beak at the front of its mouth which it used to cut leaves and stems against a cropping pad at the front of its upper jaw. Cows and sheep cut grass in much the same way, using a horny cropping pad in their upper jaw and sharp teeth instead of a beak in the lower.

The floor of *Camptosaurus*'s lower jaw had a wide groove running along it where a long tongue probably grew. The tongue pulled food into the mouth where it was chopped off by the beak and passed to the rows of teeth to be crushed and chopped into small pieces.

We know from the arrangement of the jaws and the muscles that *Camptosaurus*'s jaws moved like a pair of nutcrackers rather than with the slicing action of the flesh eaters. The most remarkable thing about the way it ate, however, was the way it used its cheeks. These bird-hipped dinosaurs were the only reptiles to develop cheeks, which today are found only in mammals. Cheeks are useful

Camptosaurus was the first of the large, two-legged, bird-hipped dinosaurs. Nearly 5 m long, it weighed 3·8 tonnes and fed on plants, grazing and browsing in large herds on the flat plains.

because they allow more food to be taken in one mouthful than most reptiles can manage. *Camptosaurus* chewed in the same way that living fruit bats do. Its elastic-sided cheeks pushed food onto its teeth so that as it chomped up and down the leaves were gradually ground down.

If food is to be held in the mouth long enough for it to be chewed into small fragments, the animal's food and air passages must be separated so that it can breathe and eat at the same time. Sixty million years before, when the paramammals had become warm-blooded, they had developed a bony palate, separating the nose passages from the mouth so that air could be taken in through the nose while food was held in the mouth. Now the same thing happened to plant-eating dinosaurs.

We know from trackways of footprints that *Camptosaurus* usually walked on its back legs, but since it had hooves on the front legs as well as the back, it must sometimes have gone on all fours. If the herd was migrating or they were being chased by a flesh eater they would have run on only two legs but if they were grazing they would have moved about on all fours.

They were also on all fours when they mated.

The female squatted down with her tail raised and twisted to one side. The male placed his front legs across her shoulders and one back leg over her hip. Then he pushed his tail under hers so that their sex organs were in contact. The male inserted his sex organ and emptied his sperm into the female. The sperm was stored in a special organ inside the female and used to fertilize the eggs as they were produced from her ovaries but before they developed their shells. One mating served to fertilize several batches of eggs.

All dinosaurs probably mated like this, with only minor differences. As with modern reptiles and birds, whose sex organs do not show on the outside, mating involved very close co-operation between the male and the female and was only successful if the female wished it to be and could let the male know that she was ready. Many animals have special courtship displays: peacocks spread their shimmering tails, crowned cranes dance, lizards arch their backs and raise their crests. Dinosaurs probably behaved in the same way. Too ponderous to dance, the female would probably have raised her tail and arched her back in a special way that the male could recognize instantly.

Like modern reptiles, male dinosaurs had no true penis. Instead they had a special organ which did not show on the outside. In order to mate, the male and female dinosaurs had to bring the undersides of their tails close together so that the male could insert his special organ into an opening in the female's body.

THE STEGOSAURS

At the very beginning of the Jurassic Period, 190 million years ago, a small bird-hipped dinosaur lived in the south of England. It was 3·7 m long and its body was covered by small, bony plates which, over the hip and down the tail, formed triangular spikes. This was *Scelidosaurus*, the ancestor of a group of dinosaurs known as the armoured dinosaurs, the stegosaurs and the ankylosaurs.

The greatest problem faced by all the plant eaters was the existence of flesh-eating dinosaurs. The sauropods took to the water to avoid them and grew to an enormous size. The ornithopods such as *Camptosaurus* were probably able to escape by running away and by grouping together in large herds. The other plant eaters developed a protective armour, a development that has been called the 'hands off trend'. All the ancestors of the dinosaurs had bony plates in their skins but many lost them as they either became more active or went to live in the swamps. Some, such as the stegosaurs, increased and improved on the original armour.

The armoured dinosaurs developed from *Scelidosaurus* in two main ways. The most dramatic-looking group, the stegosaurs, had enormous bony plates and spikes on their bodies. The other group, the ankylosaurs, developed a solid box-like carapace rather like the bony carapace of a tortoise.

The most spiky dinosaur of all was the 4·5 m long *Kentrosaurus*, from East Africa. In the middle of its back the armour stuck up as vertical plates but from the middle down to the tip of the tail there were pairs of huge spikes. The last pair was on the very tip of its tail and another spike projected sideways at the hip. These great spikes made *Kentrosaurus* very difficult to approach and most flesh eaters would have kept well away.

The strangest stegosaur of all was *Stegosaurus*, which has featured in many science fiction stories because of its extraordinary appearance. *Stegosaurus* grew to 9 m long and weighed up to 1·75 tonnes. It had a tiny head and its brain, no bigger than a walnut, weighed only 70 g. Its front legs were shorter than its back ones but it walked on all fours, with its belly well off the ground. Enormous triangular bony plates grew from its skin down the middle of its back. Behind the head they were quite small, but they grew larger and larger until over the hip they were up to a metre across. Down the tail they grew gradually smaller again. The last metre of the tail had no plates but instead, two pairs

Below: *Scelidosaurus*, the ancestor of the armoured stegosaurs and ankylosaurs, lived 190 million years ago. It was 3·7 m long and the small triangular spikes on its body are the first hint of the great spikes and plates that were to grow on its descendants.

The skeleton of *Kentrosaurus*, a 4·5 m long armoured dinosaur from East Africa, shows that its protective spikes were not extensions of the vertebrae but were fixed into the skin of its back.

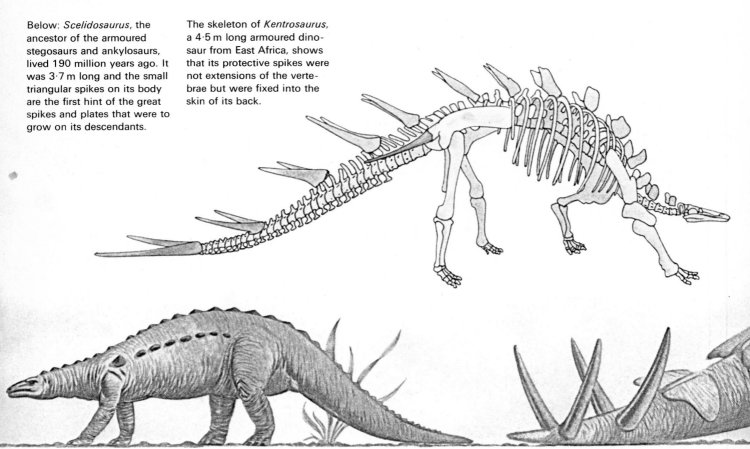

of vicious-looking spikes which would have inflicted terrible wounds on any unwary predator.

We do not know exactly what the bony plates were for, but they were probably for protection. They were arranged in pairs and are usually shown sticking straight up. This certainly looks dramatic, but in this position they would have been very ineffective and it would not have taken the flesh eaters long to discover that they were just for show. As long as they kept out of the way of the spiky tail, they could have just walked alongside and ripped *Stegosaurus* to pieces. Recently, scientists have discovered that the armour plates probably grew out sideways instead of upwards, giving *Stegosaurus* a much better chance of striking enemies approaching from the side.

The extra weight of the bony plates, which was centred over the hips and the base of the tail, helped to counterbalance the front part of the body and we now know that *Stegosaurus* could stand up on its hind legs to reach the branches of trees.

Stegosaurus is not famous just for its frightening appearance but also for the so-called second brain in its hip. At the base of its spinal cord there was a cavity large enough for a brain ten times as big as the real brain in its skull. The cavity was not, however, filled with a mass of nervous tissue like a brain but by a special gland called a glycogen gland, still seen in birds today. This gland acted as a booster, making sure that there was always an adequate supply of energy to move the huge muscles of the back legs.

The recent history of *Stegosaurus* is rather an anticlimax. The two features for which it was most famous, its upright bony armour and its 'second brain' have been shown to be quite different. However, now that we know its bony plates were not just decoration but served an important and necessary function, it seems a much more probable animal of its time. The new restorations are much more realistic and give a more accurate idea of how *Stegosaurus* looked and lived.

COASTAL PLAINS OF EAST AFRICA

During the greater part of the Jurassic Period, from 190 to 140 million years ago, extensive swamps with lush vegetation occupied vast areas of the continents. There were few mountain chains and the rivers meandered slowly across wide, flat plains. Here, where the climate was warm and wet, herds

Stegosaurus was the largest of all the stegosaurs, measuring 9 m long and weighing 1·75 tonnes. The great triangular plates fixed in its skin probably stuck out sideways to cover its back and protect its sides. It is usually shown with upright plates (inset)

and front legs bent at the elbow. In this position the plates would have given it little protection and its legs would not have been able to support the weight of its body.

of giant sauropods wallowed in and around the swamps, consuming enormous quantities of ferns and horsetail plants. The sauropods were preyed upon by such flesh eaters as *Allosaurus* and *Cerato-saurus* and the spiky, plant-eating *Stegosaurus* shared the same environment.

Large parts of North America looked like this in the Jurassic and in East Africa we know that there were similar animals in the same kind of landscape. Some of the animals were slightly different in the different continents. *Kentrosaurus*, for example, was the African version of *Stegosaurus*, with long spikes arranged in pairs over its back and down its tail, and spikes jutting sideways from behind its back legs. African sauropods, *Dicraeosaurus*, looked very like their American cousin the 25 m long *Apato-saurus*, but were much smaller, being only 13 m long and 3 m high.

Not all the African dinosaurs were smaller than their American relatives: the largest land animal of all, *Brachiosaurus* lived there. Because of its long front legs and long neck, some people have suggested that it probably reached up to feed, like a giraffe, on leaves from the tops of the trees. This was certainly possible, for we know that *Brachio-saurus* could walk on land, but it would have been much more comfortable wading in the swamps where the water could support some of its weight.

Flying in the air above the coastal plains were flocks of the long-tailed fishing pterosaurs *Rham-phorhynchus* while in the undergrowth the smallest of all the dinosaurs, the tiny *Compsognathus*, chased lizards and insects.

During the Jurassic Period the giant sauropods were at the peak of their development and they dominated the landscape in most parts of the world. After this time they gradually began to decline and their place was taken by new kinds of plant-eating, bird-hipped dinosaurs. Although they became much rarer, it was not until the very end of the Age of Dinosaurs that the great sauropods finally disappeared.

Compsognathus

Kentrosaurus

Herds of plant-eating dinosaurs lived in the swampy lowlands that are now part of East Africa. Many were very similar to animals living in North America at the same time though some differed in size.

Brachiosaurus

Rhamphorhynchus

Dicraeosaurus

THE JURASSIC LAGOONS

During the second part of the Jurassic Period, clear, shallow tropical lagoons stretched all the way from Portugal to France and into southern Germany. The fine, white limestone mud they left behind hardened into rock called lithographic limestone, because it was used in a printing process called lithography. In the nineteenth century, perfectly preserved fossils were often found in the quarries.

The first bird, *Archaeopteryx*, was found in Bavaria in 1861 and in 1972 a new form of the tiny *Compsognathus* was discovered near Nice in Southern France. Instead of having three free, long fingers like all the other coelurosaurs, its fingers were joined together to form paddles. This variety of *Compsognathus* was probably specially adapted for

Fossil skeleton of the first bird, *Archaeopteryx*, from the Jurassic lagoons in Bavaria. Only five *Archaeopteryx* skeletons have so far been found. This was the second and is particularly important because it has not only wing and tail feathers like a bird but also teeth like a reptile.

Fossils found in the Jurassic lagoons show the many different kinds of animals that were alive there 150 million years ago.

Rhamphorhynchus

Pterodactylus

Crocodile

Compsognathus

Tortoise

King crab

Compsognathus corallestris

swimming and diving, and fed on the crabs and other crustaceans that lived in the lagoons.

The lithographic limestone is not important only because these two remarkable animals were found there, but because it contains all kinds of animal life from in, above and beside the lagoons.

Jellyfish stranded on the beach are beautifully preserved, in spite of the fact that they had no hard parts; ammonites are there and king crab tracks, with, at the end of the track, the king crab itself. Fishes, crayfish, crabs and other crustaceans prove that there was ample food in the lagoons to supply the needs of many different animals. Marine crocodiles fed on the many varieties of fish and marine turtles flourished.

On the edges of the lagoons, dragonflies and other insects fluttered along, preyed on by many different kinds of lizard, which in turn were hunted by *Archaeopteryx* and *Compsognathus*. All the modern groups of lizard were there, and in some areas the scenery and animal life must have looked quite modern. Some of the larger flesh-eating coeluro-saurs such as *Ornitholestes* may have been there, feeding on *Archaeopteryx* and other small reptiles.

While all this hunting, scavenging and feeding was taking place on the ground, the air was dominated by pterosaurs. The larger ones swooped down, diving onto fish in the lagoon, while the smaller ones such as *Pterodactylus* caught insects in the air.

Throughout the whole Age of Dinosaurs, only the lithographic limestone contains a complete record, enabling us to reconstruct in great detail the varied animal life of 150 million years ago.

Ornitholestes

Archaeopteryx

Lizard

JURASSIC MARINE REPTILES

The Jurassic seas were dominated by the ichthyosaurs or 'fish lizards'. No-one yet knows how ichthyosaurs evolved. Though they may have been descended from land-dwelling reptiles, by the beginning of the Triassic they had returned to the seas and lost their ability to move on land.

The ichthyosaur's overall shape was like a fish, and it ranged from 1 to 12 m in length. Its limbs had changed to fin-like paddles, and it had a tail fin and a large, triangular fin in the middle of its back. Its head had a long, narrow, pointed snout, with numerous sharp teeth.

When fossil skeletons were first found, their tails always seemed to be bent or broken in the same place. Later it was discovered that this was not a break, but a support for the large tail fin, which had no bones in its upper part and so had not been preserved. During the last century a large number of complete skeletons were found in Holzmaden in Württemberg, Germany. Several of these had the outline of skin preserved with them, showing the exact details of the fins and paddles. The skin was in such good condition that even the pigment cells which give colour were preserved, and we now know that some ichthyosaurs' backs were a tortoise-shell colour — dark, russet brown.

An ichthyosaur's front paddles were twice as long as its back ones. Inside were arm and leg bones similar to those of land-dwelling reptiles, with shoulder and hip and elbow and knee joints. There was a thick layer of flesh around the bones at the posterior-edge so that the paddle was thick at the front, but thinner and flatter at the back, like an aeroplane or a penguin wing.

Other skeletons from Holzmaden proved that ichthyosaurs gave birth to live young, for some had as many as four small skeletons preserved inside them. If these had been swallowed by the adults, they would have been digested and destroyed, so they could only have been embryos developing inside the mother's body. The final proof of this came when a fossil was found which showed the mother and her young at the moment of birth.

The ichthyosaurs were divided into two groups. The first had long, narrow limbs or paddles, ending in five many-jointed fingers. The second, more successful group, had shorter, broader paddles with up to nine stumpy fingers on each one. In both groups the paddles were stiff and could only move at the shoulder and elbow joints, but the broader

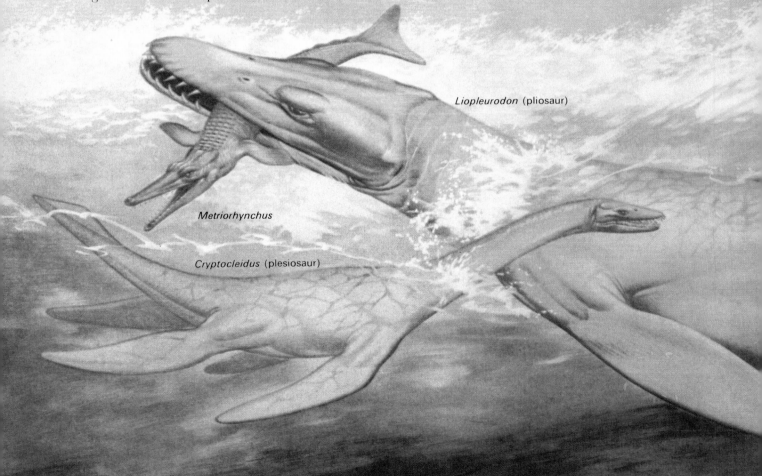

Liopleurodon (pliosaur)

Metriorhynchus

Cryptocleidus (plesiosaur)

paddles of the second group were better shaped for movement through the water.

Coprolites or fossil droppings have been found with the ichthyosaur skeletons, some still inside the animals. The main content of the coprolites are scales and spines from a fast-moving surface-water fish called *Pholidophorus*. They show that ichthyosaurs were active fish hunters, swimming and feeding near or at the surface of the sea.

Fossilized stomach contents of other ichthyosaurs give a rather different impression. Many specimens contain a mass of tiny, black, curved hooks, each measuring 1 to 2 mm in length. One young ichthyosaur, less than 1·5 m long, had about 478,000 of these hooks in its stomach.

The hooks came from the tentacles of cephalopods, relatives of the squid and octopus. Each cephalopod had ten tentacles with about thirty hooks on each. So this particular ichthyosaur had eaten approximately 1590 cephalopods. The hooks do not appear in the droppings, but probably accumulated in the stomach, to be spat out later on. Today sperm whales, which also feed on cephalopods, do the same thing. Some of the later ichthyosaurs lost their teeth and probably fed almost exclusively on cephalopods, grabbing them with their toothless jaws and swallowing them whole.

After the Jurassic, the ichthyosaurs became less important in the sea, which is surprising because

Ichthyosaurs, plesiosaurs and pliosaurs were the main reptiles of the Jurassic seas. Though they lived in the same environment they did not compete, for they ate different kinds of food.

Ichthyosaurus

This young ichthyosaur has been so well preserved that even the impression of its skin can be seen. It also clearly shows the tail and back fin and the hydrofoil shape of the flippers. Over 150 million years ago the dead ichthyosaur sank in mud at the bottom of the sea where it lay undisturbed and where lack of oxygen prevented it from decaying completely.

they seemed the best adapted of all reptiles for sea life.

Two groups of marine crocodiles flourished in the Jurassic seas. One, the only group of archosaurs to become fully water-dwelling, died out at the beginning of the Cretaceous Period. The other group survived in the seas around the African continent for much longer, finally disappearing in the Middle Eocene, 46 million years ago and 18 million years after the end of the Age of Dinosaurs.

The third group of successful marine reptiles was the plesiosaurs. At first glance they seem much less well-adapted for life in the seas than the ichthyosaurs but in fact they were to become more successful.

The plesiosaurs were descended from the same group as the nothosaurs, the reptiles which had been so important in the sea and on the shore during the Triassic Period. Plesiosaurs had wider bodies than nothosaurs, with shorter tails. Their limbs had changed to paddles, though they still had fingers and toes. Fish eaters, they had a long neck, small head and a great many sharp teeth.

At the beginning of the Jurassic some of the plesiosaurs developed longer heads and rather shorter necks. These were the ancestors of yet another group, the pliosaurs, which had become firmly established by the middle of the Jurassic Period, and were to become the largest of all marine reptiles. Pliosaurs had short thick necks with enormous heads which made up a quarter of the entire length of the body. One, *Liopleurodon*, from England, had a skull 3 m long though the overall length of its body would not have been more

The long-necked plesiosaurs were fast, agile swimmers. Their paddles acted like oars, and could move both backwards and forwards, enabling them to make sharp turns and to move rapidly through the water. Though they were highly manoeuvrable, they could not raise their paddles above the level of the shoulders and hips, so they could not dive for their food. Instead, they must have spent their time fishing in surface waters, using their long, flexible neck to reach down into the water for fish.

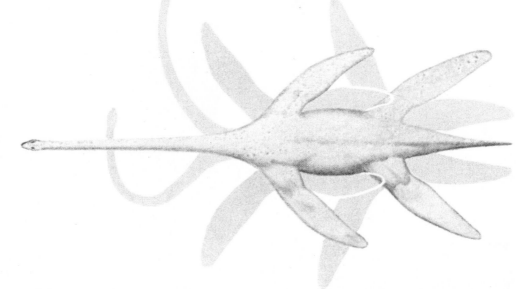

than 12 m. Their strong jaws contained massive teeth, much larger than those of a plesiosaur.

Pliosaurs were much more streamlined in shape than the long-necked plesiosaurs but though they lived in the same environment, they did not compete directly for food. Plesiosaurs concentrated on fishing and we know from the stomach contents of the short-necked pliosaurs that they ate mainly cephalopods. Both groups continued until the very end of the Cretaceous Period.

Swimming Plesiosaurs and pliosaurs not only had different shapes and different diets, they also swam in different ways. The long-necked plesiosaurs were fast, agile and highly manoeuvrable while the heavier, short-necked pliosaurs were powerful, long-distance swimmers.

Normally a swimming animal moves forward in the water when it thrusts its limbs backwards. In plesiosaurs the muscles which pulled the paddles forwards were almost as strong as those that drew them back so that they could move their limbs equally strongly in both directions. If it moved all its limbs forwards, a plesiosaur would simply swim backwards, but if it moved one forwards in a back stroke and one back in a normal swimming stroke, it could make a very sudden turn.

Plesiosaurs could not raise their paddles above the level of their shoulder joints, and so could not dive down after their food. The paddles moved as solid units, without being able to bend, and although they could make rapid flicks, they could not make powerful, sustained swimming strokes. Their oar-like action was basically a rather in-efficient way of swimming, though it suited their way of life well enough. Plesiosaurs spent most of their time paddling in the surface waters, twisting and turning in their search for food. The long neck moved in the water like a snake, but it could not make sudden turns like the body. When it was darting about looking for fish, the plesiosaur kept its long neck out of the water, stabbing its head down like a fishing bird when it sighted food.

The streamlined shape of the pliosaurs, with their large heads and thick necks, shows that they were powerful, long-distance swimmers. They used their flippers to propel them through the water and though they could not make the rapid flicking and backing strokes of the plesiosaurs, they could take long, steady strokes and they could dive in search of their cephalopod food.

The pliosaurs moved their front flippers in exactly the same way as a penguin uses its wings to 'fly' through the water. We know from skin impressions that the flippers were shaped like hydrofoils, curved outwards on the top and flat underneath. This is a most effective shape in the water. The pliosaur made a downward swimming stroke and because of the flipper's special hydrofoil shape, the pressure of water brought it back upwards ready for the next stroke, with no further effort from the animal.

The back flippers moved differently, being pulled into the body, then twisted out and drawn forwards to make the next stroke. Today, large ocean-going turtles swim in a very similar way, using their front flippers like hydrofoils, but moving their back ones rather differently.

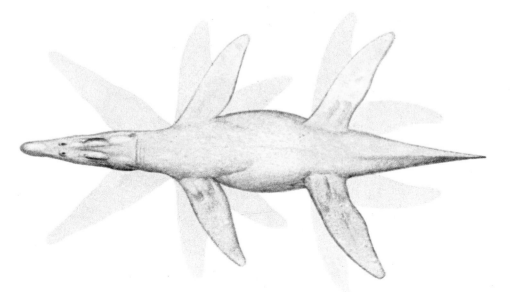

Short-necked plesiosaurs or pliosaurs were not as manoeuvrable as their long-necked relatives but were powerful, long-distance swimmers. Their front paddles moved like the 'wing' of a penguin, pushing downwards and backwards against the water. At the end of the stroke the hydrofoil-shaped paddle rose automatically, pushed up by water pressure from below. It was pulled forwards by the muscles that controlled the stroke. The main thrust of the back flippers came when they were pulled in towards the body. At the end of the stroke they were twisted so that only a narrow edge resisted the flow of water, and drawn forwards.

The Cretaceous Period – 136 to 64 million years ago

The Cretaceous was a Period of great change, during which the pattern of the modern world was firmly set. It was during this time that the dinosaurs were at their most numerous and most varied. Almost all the groups that had become established during the Jurassic survived but whereas the Jurassic had been dominated by the lizard-hipped saurischians – the heavy carnosaurs and sauropods and the lightly-built coelurosaurs – the Cretaceous was the time of the bird-hipped ornithischians.

At the beginning of the Cretaceous, 136 million years ago, there was little sign of the changes that were to come. The climate was unchanged and it was still warm and wet throughout most of the world. The large sauropods were still the main plant eaters and the flesh eaters were almost exactly like their Jurassic forebears. The plant life seemed to be typically Jurassic. Nevertheless there were suggestions of future developments. The armoured stegosaurs had vanished and their place had been taken by an even more heavily protected group of bird-hipped dinosaurs, the squat ankylosaurs. Even the flesh eaters, usually slow to change, evolved new ways of dealing with their prey. One bird-hipped group, the ornithopods, which had been relatively unimportant in the Jurassic, was beginning to increase.

In the middle of the Cretaceous, 100 million years ago, major geological changes occurred: the final break-up of the continents began. North America split from Europe although it still remained firmly connected to Asia. Antarctica and Australia parted and the subcontinent of India broke away from Africa and Australia. The last geological event was the opening up of the South Atlantic. A thin arm of sea gradually spread from the north and the south until a narrow strip of water was formed, rather like the present-day Red Sea. From this point on, South America and Africa gradually drifted further and further apart. The narrow connection between Africa and Europe was also severed and by the middle of the Cretaceous Period all the modern continents had their own separate existence for the first time.

The separation of the continents had an important effect on the dinosaurs. They were now cut off from one another on different land masses and could no longer migrate from one region to another. During the Triassic and the Jurassic, dinosaurs had been much the same all over the world. Now that they were isolated from one another, they began to respond in different ways to the changes in their environments.

In fact, throughout the southern continents there was hardly any change. The main plant eaters were still the giant sauropods and these were still preyed on by the great carnosaurs. There is little evidence of any evolution among the southern dinosaurs: they simply managed to survive until the end of the Cretaceous and that was all.

On the northern continents the situation was entirely different, and there is abundant evidence of a rapidly evolving population of ever more successful dinosaurs. The most dramatic developments were among the plant-eating, bird-hipped dinosaurs, the ornithopods. These evolved into an enormous variety of forms from the duck-billed dinosaurs (the hadrosaurs) to the bone-heads and a great number of different horned dinosaurs (the ceratopsians).

The sauropods managed to survive on the northern continents but were gradually driven from their habitats by the ornithopods. The flesh eaters continued as before but even they showed changes: some of the coelurosaurs stopped eating only other animals and began to take a mixed diet of meat and plants. The ankylosaurs evolved into a number of different types with different patterns of armour and different kinds of tail with bony spikes or heavy clubs on the end.

Left: The new plants that
evolved in the warm
Cretaceous climate included
flowering varieties. New trees,
including oak, cinnamon,
magnolia, plane, laurel and
giant redwood appeared.
Older conifers and monkey
puzzle trees remained.

During the Cretaceous Period
the continents finally separated
into their modern pattern.
South and North America
were linked for the first time
since the Triassic, though they
separated again immediately
after the Age of Dinosaurs.
There were few mountain
chains. Most of the land was
flat, and warm, clear seas
spread over vast areas.

Towards the end of the Cretaceous Period, South and North America were joined for the first time since the Triassic, over 150 million years before, and several of the newly evolved northern dinosaurs moved south. So far as we know, the three main groups, the ceratopsians, hadrosaurs and ankylosaurs did not reach any of the other southern continents.

The changes that occurred among the northern dinosaurs were influenced by important changes in the plant life of the Period. In the south the plants seem to have remained much as they had been at the beginning of the Cretaceous but in the north, modern flowering plants spread everywhere. The new plants were much more fibrous than the old and contained a substance called silica. The dinosaurs had to make special adaptations to enable them to use the new plants as food and because they were able to do this quickly they were able to survive and even to become more successful than ever.

The great earthquakes, volcanic eruptions and tidal waves that must have accompanied the break-up of the continents had failed to destroy the dinosaurs and the changes in plant life had had little effect. At the end of the Cretaceous, 64 million years ago, another crisis came. We do not know what kind of crisis this was but by the end of the Period, dinosaurs of all kinds had totally disappeared from the world.

MODERN PLANTS AND ANIMALS

The plant life of the later part of the Cretaceous Period would have been quite familiar to us, for as well as the ancient sequoia, ginkgo and conifers most of the common trees, shrubs and flowers of today were already growing. There were pines and firs, oaks, ash, poplars, sycamores, willows, maples and birch. The breadfruit tree and fig tree which are now only found in warmer countries were mixed in with these. The dense undergrowth of shrubs and small trees contained magnolia bushes, viburnum, cinnamon, laurel, and myrtus as well as witch hazel and dogwood. One of the more surprising plants was holly. Many of the common flowers of our gardens were to be seen: climbing roses, polygonums, grape vines and passion flowers. Banks of saxifrage formed colourful patches with lilies, primulas, euphorbias and heather.

The flowering plants added a blaze of colour to the Cretaceous scene and there were scents in the air. Brightly-coloured flowers and flower scents were connected with another aspect of life in the Cretaceous for it was then that the social insects, the termites and the bees, appeared. Bees and other insects, attracted by the bright colours and the scents of the flowers, carried pollen from one to another just as they do today.

The water plants included the modern floating fern *Salvinia*, known as the Kariba weed, *Pistia*, the water lettuce and *Trapa*, the water chestnut. There were even waterlilies. On the water and along the edges of the lakes and swampy marshes were new varieties of birds, all of which would be recognizable today.

The fossil record of birds shows far more sea and water birds than any other kind. This is because bird bones are very fragile and are more likely to be preserved in sand and mud than anywhere else. Most modern bird skeletons are very alike, as they are all basically adapted for flight. It is very difficult to identify a particular bird family from an odd fragment of, for example, a leg bone. In spite of these problems, members of modern bird families have been discovered in Cretaceous rocks in many parts of the world, especially in North America.

The two Cretaceous birds most often seen in pictures of life a hundred million years ago are *Hesperornis* and *Ichthyornis*. *Hesperornis* was a toothed, swimming fish eater which had lost its power of flight. *Ichthyornis* was a highly-developed, fast flyer, rather like a modern tern. Both these families became extinct in the Cretaceous but before the Period ended 64 million years ago, several other modern birds were already living in a wide variety of habitats.

The fishing cormorant *Graculavus* would have been seen diving onto fish and sitting drying out its wings in the sun. Divers such as *Lonchodytes* swam on the surface of the water, diving down from time to time to hunt for fish. Striding in the shallows a stork or heron-like bird, *Plegadornis*, hunted frogs, fish and water beetles. Swimming along the edge of the water and walking on the banks were the rails, *Telmatornis*, looking very like modern rails and moorhens. They fed mainly on insects and worms, but also took seeds, berries and water plants. Groups of long-legged waders, *Palaeotringa*, walked up and down the muddy shores, probing the mud for worms, insects and small shellfish. In the trees away from the water the occasional owl would be roosting. The open shallow waters were full of flamingos, feeding on algae in the water.

During the Cretaceous dinosaurs reached the high point of their evolution but important changes were also taking place among other groups of reptiles. The lizards continued to evolve and the snakes appeared in Africa in the form of primitive pythons. The first snakes lived in the water and probably lost their limbs and developed their serpentine movement as a way of swimming. There is no evidence of any poisonous snakes in the Cretaceous.

Among the turtles, the marsh turtles and terrapins flourished and modern land tortoises plodded around eating vegetation. Crocodiles still occupied their ancient place in the economy of nature.

In the sea the ichthyosaurs and plesiosaurs continued and were joined by giant marine lizards – relatives of the monitor lizard, the great Komodo dragon of today. The main change was the rapid evolution of fast-swimming, modern bony fishes, the ancestors of the herring and salmon.

Finally the mammals began to evolve into modern groups, including the ancestors of the possums, shrews and hedgehogs, cat- and dog-like flesh eaters and primates. The first fossil primate

is *Purgatorius*, a small, shrew-like animal rather like the tree shrew *Tupaia* from South-East Asia.

With all these modern plants and animals appearing, it is as if the modern world had established itself with complete disregard for the giant dinosaurs. Dinosaurs were of little importance to the birds, lizards, snakes and mammals of the time. They certainly did not compete directly with them for food or space and the majority of animals at the end of the Cretaceous would have paid little attention to them.

During the second part of the Cretaceous Period, animal and plant life looked in some ways very modern. Already many different types of bird had appeared: there were owls, rails, cormorants, waders and tern-like sea birds. Small flowering plants such as roses evolved and trees such as oak and holly were common. The new flowers were pollinated by bees and other insects while lizards, snakes and small mammals abounded in the thick undergrowth. Yet in this same, modern landscape lived the dinosaurs, now at the very peak of their evolutionary success, with both new and old types flourishing.

FLESH-EATING DINOSAURS

During the Cretaceous Period the great lizard-hipped flesh eaters, the carnosaurs, continued to roam over the plains and lowlands. Like the giant plant-eaters they preyed on, they grew even larger than before. The biggest, *Tyrannosaurus rex* was almost 15 m long, considerably bigger than its Jurassic ancestor *Allosaurus*.

The frightening-looking flesh eaters such as *Tyrannosaurus* and its relatives *Albertosaurus* from Canada and *Tarbosaurus* from Mongolia, could never have been very agile. They needed a great deal of food and energy to move their heavy bodies about. If they ran about too much they became overheated and had to stop to cool off. Slow, ponderous walking, with short bursts of faster movement was all they were able to manage.

Their main weapons were their massive, cruelly-clawed feet, which could rip open any unprotected plant-eating dinosaur. The meat from one kill would last for weeks. A 10 tonne flesh eater like *Tyrannosaurus* would have been able to live on half a 20 tonne sauropod or 3 smaller duck-billed dinosaurs for a whole year.

This means that the carnosaurs probably shared their prey, feeding until they were satisfied, then lying bloated and drowsy for days on end until it was time to go in search of another meal. During the Cretaceous we know that there were many thousands of plant-eating dinosaurs. Even if the flesh eaters ate only the bodies of plant eaters that had died naturally, there would have been enough meat for them all and they would not have needed to do much active hunting.

The largest, most frightening of the flesh eaters was *Tyrannosaurus rex*. It is usually shown as nearly 15 m long and 6 m high, standing up on its strong back legs. Its long tail drags on the ground and its enormous mouth is open, showing long, dagger-like teeth ready to tear its victim to pieces. Sometimes it is shown fighting other dinosaurs. By any standards it seems the most sensational predator seen on earth.

Recently, scientists have discovered that it was not quite as alarming as it looked. Its tail was shorter, and it did not stand so high because most of the time it held its backbone horizontally, parallel to the ground, with its tail straight out behind. From footprints we know that *Tyrannosaurus*'s massive hind legs took short steps, only about 1 m long, so that it waddled along rather like a goose, its front legs dangling far above the ground.

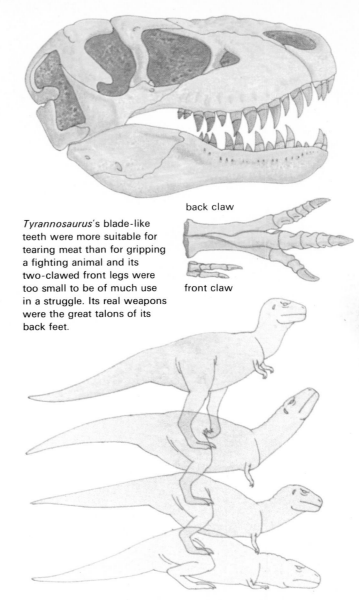

back claw

Tyrannosaurus's blade-like teeth were more suitable for tearing meat than for gripping a fighting animal and its two-clawed front legs were too small to be of much use in a struggle. Its real weapons were the great talons of its back feet.

front claw

Tyrannosaurus's tiny front legs had massive shoulder muscles which helped to raise its heavy body when it had been lying down. Its two-pronged front legs probably pushed firmly into the ground so that when it stretched its back legs to stand up it did not slide forwards. By tossing its heavy head back as its front legs left the ground, it would have brought its centre of gravity closer to its back legs, to prevent it from toppling forward. Once standing, the weight of its tail balanced the weight of its head and body.

Tyrannosaurus rex was the largest flesh eater of all time. Almost 15 m long and weighing 10 tonnes, it preyed on the vulnerable plant eaters on the plains and at the edges of the swamps. The flesh eaters grew gradually larger to keep pace with the increasing size of their prey. Giants such as *Tyrannosaurus*, *Tarbosaurus* and *Albertosaurus* had probably reached the maximum possible size: if they had been any larger and heavier, they would no longer have been able to walk on two legs and would not have been able to hunt effectively.

Even its vicious-looking teeth were not as bad as they seemed: if it had tried to tackle living animals, the teeth would have snapped off in the struggle. However, the great claws on its three-toed feet were effective weapons against even the largest plant eaters and the teeth were probably only used to feed on dead animals.

Its tiny front legs, which had only two fingers, were used as toothpicks to clean off bits of meat stuck between its teeth. They also had another important function – they helped *Tyrannosaurus* to get up when it had been lying down. When *Tyrannosaurus* lay or sat down, its legs were folded up and its belly and chest rested on the ground. If it simply stretched its back legs to get up, it would only have pushed itself along like a giant armless lizard. However, with its two-clawed fingers stuck firmly into the ground, it was able to straighten its back legs without slithering and sliding forward on its belly and so lift its heavy body up. At the same time it threw its head back, putting most of the weight of the front of the body over its hips so that it did not topple forward again.

Though the flesh-eating dinosaurs probably did not have to hunt very vigorously for their food, there must have been times when they needed to move faster than usual to catch their prey. In the subtropical climate of the Cretaceous, overheating was a serious problem, for it meant that large dinosaurs had to stop frequently to cool off. One flesh eater developed a built-in cooling system which helped it to remain more active, in spite of its large size. *Spinosaurus*, from Egypt, was 12 m long. Long spikes grew from the vertebrae of its backbone giving it a huge, fan-like sail over its back. The sail was covered by skin and was supplied by hundreds of blood vessels, veins and arteries.

The sail worked in the same way as the early paramammal sails over 100 million years earlier. In the heat of the day *Spinosaurus* could turn head-on to the sun. Only a thin edge of the sail would be directly exposed, while the side provided a large surface for heat loss. By turning the sail sideways towards the sun in the early morning, *Spinosaurus* could quickly increase its internal temperature and become active before other reptiles had fully

One of the most curious dinosaurs of the Cretaceous Period was *Spinosaurus*, a 12 m long flesh eater from Egypt. The skin-covered sail on its back was supported by bony spikes, some as much as 1.9 m long. The sail helped *Spinosaurus* to lose excess heat and probably meant that it could move about more quickly than other large flesh eaters of its time.

adjusted to the temperature changes and awoken from their normal drowsiness.

Unlike the other large flesh eaters, *Spinosaurus* had strong front legs. Its back legs were still its most important weapons and it could stand on these to fight as the other carnosaurs did. But walking on four legs does not use up as much energy as walking on two, and when it was wandering in search of food, it would go on all fours.

Though *Spinosaurus* could have been more active than the other carnosaurs, its delicate spine would soon have been torn to pieces in fierce fighting. Like the other ponderous, ambling flesh eaters it probably hunted lazily, choosing out animals it could easily overcome or feeding on plant eaters that had already died.

THE CLAWED DINOSAURS

All the large flesh eaters used the claws on their back feet to kill their prey but in two flesh eaters, one small and one large, the claws developed into especially effective weapons. The most dangerous dinosaur of all was probably not the giant, ponderous *Tyrannosaurus* but a small form which stood only 1 m high and was only 2·5 m from head to tail, about the size of a small pony. Its name is *Deinonychus* or 'terrible claw'.

Deinonychus was the most agile of all the dinosaurs. It leaped at its victims, slashing their necks and tearing out their entrails with a speed unknown in the world of reptiles. It did not use its teeth or its front claws for this, but a single, enormous sickle-shaped toe claw. Other flesh eaters walked on all three toes, but 'terrible claw' used only two, keeping the inner, clawed toe well off the ground so that it never became worn down from walking.

Standing on one leg, *Deinonychus* swung its claw in a great arc, and it could also have jumped onto its prey. Today Australian cassowaries have a sharp spike on their second toe which they use as a defence when an enemy approaches too close. As a hunter, *Deinonychus* had to take its prey by surprise, closing in with tremendous speed and slashing out with its claws before the animal had a chance to escape.

Because it had to stand on one leg to fight,

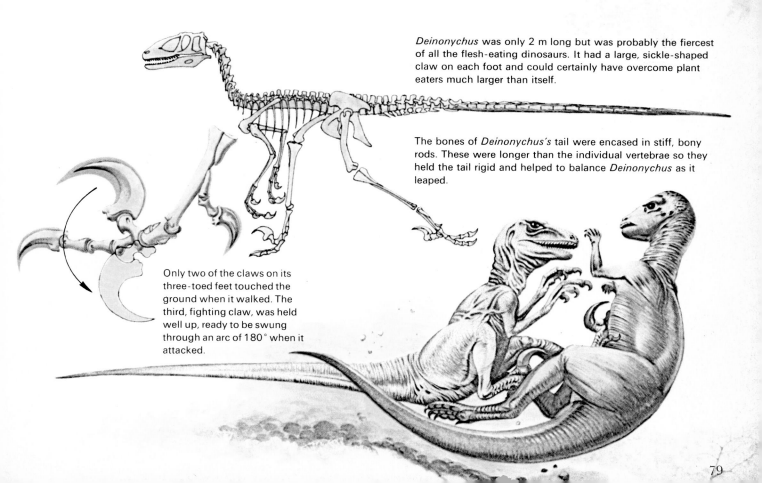

Deinonychus was only 2 m long but was probably the fiercest of all the flesh-eating dinosaurs. It had a large, sickle-shaped claw on each foot and could certainly have overcome plant eaters much larger than itself.

The bones of *Deinonychus's* tail were encased in stiff, bony rods. These were longer than the individual vertebrae so they held the tail rigid and helped to balance *Deinonychus* as it leaped.

Only two of the claws on its three-toed feet touched the ground when it walked. The third, fighting claw, was held well up, ready to be swung through an arc of 180° when it attacked.

Deinonychus needed a very good sense of balance. To help it to remain steady, its tail was specially strengthened with thin rods of bone. Part of each tail joint was extended into a rod as long as ten separate vertebrae. The chevron bones, small wedge-shaped bones underneath the vertebrae, were also lengthened so that each tail bone was encased in about 40 stiff, bony rods. The tail was therefore very stiff and though it could move up and down freely, it could not twist sideways.

Deinonychus had three, long-clawed fingers on its hands and its wrists were much more mobile than any other dinosaur's wrists. Its hands could be used for grappling with its wounded prey and for pulling off flesh torn by its terrible back claws. With its speed and slashing power, *Deinonychus* must have been the most formidable creature of the Age of Dinosaurs.

In Mongolia another type of flesh-eating dinosaur has been found, also armed with terrible claws – this time not one on each foot but three on each hand. It had forelimbs that were 2·5 m long, longer than *Deinonychus*' whole body, and it is named appropriately *Deinocheirus* or 'terrible hand'. Unfortunately the rest of its body has not yet been found, so we have no real idea what it looked like. We know that its long front legs were not used for walking and that it must therefore have stood high on its back legs so that they did not reach the ground. It is reasonable to guess that it stood and walked like all the other large flesh eaters and that its head was probably also much the same. But this *is* just guesswork. The only evidence we have is a pair of enormous arms that were clearly capable of inflicting terrible wounds.

With such long front claws, *Deinocheirus* must have been a large dinosaur and an active killer. It was adapted for attacking from the front, with a slashing, ripping action. The three-clawed fingers could splay out but they were usually kept close together while the arms swung forwards in an arc from its sides. It could swing both arms together or it could strike at an animal's neck with the right and left hand alternately. First it would try to cut the animal's neck veins or to rip open its soft underbelly. Then it would use its hands and feet to tear the body literally to pieces.

Because only the arm has been found, we do not know whether *Deinocheirus* was an unusual carnosaur or a giant version of a coelurosaur. If it was a coelurosaur its habits must have been very different from the rest of these small dinosaurs. Until further discoveries are made, this must remain unsolved.

These enormous arms are all that has so far been found of a dinosaur called *Deinocheirus* or 'terrible hand'. The 2·5 m arms were found in Mongolia, where many other important discoveries have recently been made. Until more of its skeleton is uncovered we can only guess what *Deinocheirus* looked like but it is certain that it was a giant flesh eater and that it must have been one of the most dangerous dinosaurs of the Cretaceous Period.

THE SMALL FLESH EATERS

The small, flesh-eating coelurosaurs survived and flourished in the Cretaceous Period. Like the other groups of dinosaurs, new forms evolved with new ways of life.

One of these, *Ornithomimus*, looked rather like a modern ostrich and for a flesh-eating dinosaur its appearance seems to be out of character. Its skull was extremely small compared to its body. It had a bird-like beak with no teeth and long, thin, rather bird-like legs. It had three long, slender fingers on each hand and a very long neck. The structure of its arm was very similar to the large arm of *Deinocheirus*, but it must obviously have lived in a different way.

Many new kinds of these advanced coelurosaurs evolved so we know that their way of life was a successful one, though we can tell from their skeletons that it was very different from that of the other small flesh eaters. They had no claws to tear flesh and no teeth to chew it. They had no way of defending themselves from other reptiles and could survive only by avoiding their enemies. Their long, thin legs show that they were fast runners and they

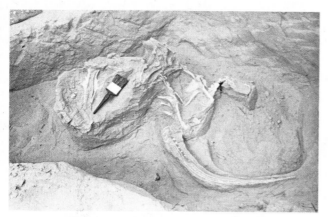

A unique fossil from Mongolia: a small plant eater, *Protoceratops*, being attacked by the flesh eater *Velociraptor*.

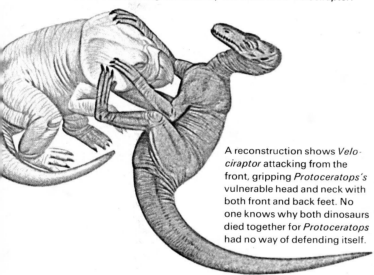

A reconstruction shows *Velociraptor* attacking from the front, gripping *Protoceratops's* vulnerable head and neck with both front and back feet. No one knows why both dinosaurs died together for *Protoceratops* had no way of defending itself.

Its large neck had huge muscles but no bony protection and its beak was adapted for cutting tough plants, not for fighting.

The ostrich-like *Ornithomimus* was a coelurosaur, a specially adapted descendant of the small flesh eaters that had evolved right at the beginning of the age of Dinosaurs. *Ornithomimus* was 4 m long, larger than many of the other coelurosaurs. Like its ancestors it still ate small lizards and mammals but it also fed on plants and probably stole dinosaur eggs.

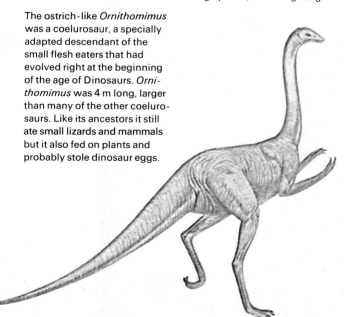

probably avoided predators simply by running away from them.

People have argued for a long time about their long, thin hands, about how they used them and what they used them for. The theory used to be that they were for handling objects and some people consider that *Ornithomimus* was an egg stealer. As if to prove this, skeletons have been found on top of a nest of dinosaur eggs, killed in the act of stealing.

Though *Ornithomimus* may have eaten eggs, its hands were not really suitable for carrying them about. It is more likely that it used its hands for scooping the sand away to expose the nests of eggs. It then broke the eggs with its beak and sucked out the contents.

In many ways *Ornithomimus* was like an ostrich with a long tail and with no feathers. With its long flexible neck it could reach the ground while still standing and could dart its head here and there just like a bird. Some people think that it fed on insects, snapping them up with its darting bill but as it was 4 m long, as big as a family car, it is hard to imagine that it could catch enough insects to keep it alive. The only food there was plenty of at the time was plant material and it may have eaten plants as well as insects and eggs. In its search for food it would have used its hand to disturb the undergrowth: anything that scuttled out or jumped up – insects, small lizards and small, furry mammals – would have been snapped up by a sudden stab of the beak.

Ornithomimus and its relatives are always counted as flesh-eating dinosaurs, but in reality they were descendants of flesh eaters that had changed their way of life to become mainly vegetarian.

As well as looking like ostriches, they also lived the same kind of life as ostriches and game birds do today. Although they could not fly, they could escape from enemies by running off at high speed. They had no direct competitor in the dinosaur world and they survived right up to the end of the Age of Dinosaurs.

The normal flesh-eating coelurosaurs were still living at the same time and there is a remarkable example of one, *Velociraptor*, that died or was killed just as it was attacking the plant eater *Protoceratops*. The entwined skeletons of these two dinosaurs, with *Velociraptor's* hands round the head of *Protoceratops*, were discovered during the Joint Polish–Mongolian Expedition to the Gobi desert in 1971. This is the only known record of a dinosaur fight. Before this discovery we could only guess that they must have taken place.

THE ANKYLOSAURS

During the Cretaceous an enormous variety of bird-hipped dinosaurs evolved, all of which were plant eaters. Some giant lizard-hipped sauropods survived but they were less important and less numerous than the new bird-hipped forms. With the large numbers of different kinds of lizard-hipped flesh eaters, the peaceful vegetarians found themselves in a very dangerous situation. Two groups, both descended from the early Jurassic *Scelidosaurus*, concentrated not on escape or on living away from flesh eaters but on protective armour.

The first group, the stegosaurs, grew pairs of spiky plates and these were, as we have seen, successful only during the Jurassic Period. The second group, the ankylosaurs, were like giant spiky tortoises, covered with a thick layer of bone. Unlike the stegosaurs, they survived until the end of the Cretaceous Period.

Acanthopholis was an early type of ankylosaur and came from southern England. It was about 4 m long and its back was covered with thick bony plates, slightly hinged along the crosswise rows so that it could arch its back. In many ways it looked like a large version of *Scelidosaurus*. Another, also from England, *Polacanthus*, seemed half way between a stegosaur and an ankylosaur. It was 4·7 m long and had large conical spines running in pairs from behind its head to the middle of its back. The largest ones were above the shoulder and it had a set of bony triangles running down its tail. The spines make it look like a stegosaur but its hip region was like an ankylosaur, completely covered by a solid bony corset, patterned with small, rounded lumps of bone.

Ankylosaurus, which gave ankylosaurs their name, is now called *Euoplocephalus*. It was like a living tank: 5 m long, only half the length of the spiky *Stegosaurus*, it weighed 3 tonnes, twice as much. The top of its head was covered in a thick bony shield and from the neck to the tip of its tail it had large, ridged plates of bone. The ridges of each plate grew into a short spike and at the end of its tail a bony club, like the mace of a medieval knight, formed its only real weapon.

Like the spiky stegosaurs, ankylosaurs grew armour to protect themselves. The skeleton of *Euoplocephalus* (left) shows that it had a normal spine, with long back legs and a heavy tail. The bony plates that formed a protective blanket over its back were fixed in the skin, making it look rather like a giant tortoise.

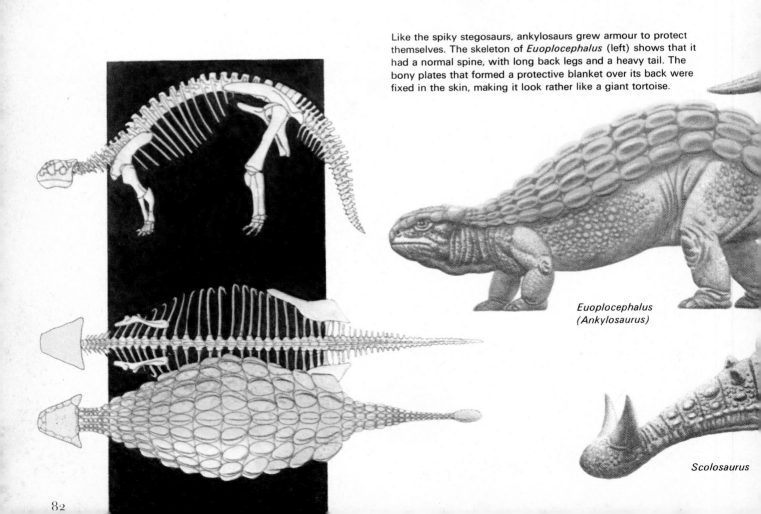

Euoplocephalus
(*Ankylosaurus*)

Scolosaurus

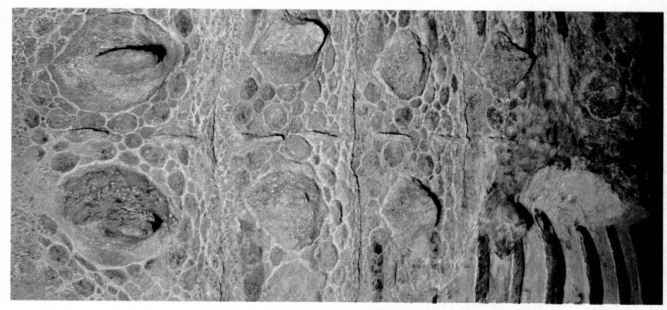

Part of the bony carapace of the only known specimen of
Scolosaurus cutleri, a large ankylosaur weighing 3·5 tonnes.
Thick spikes grew out from the hard surface, giving extra
protection to the soft body underneath.

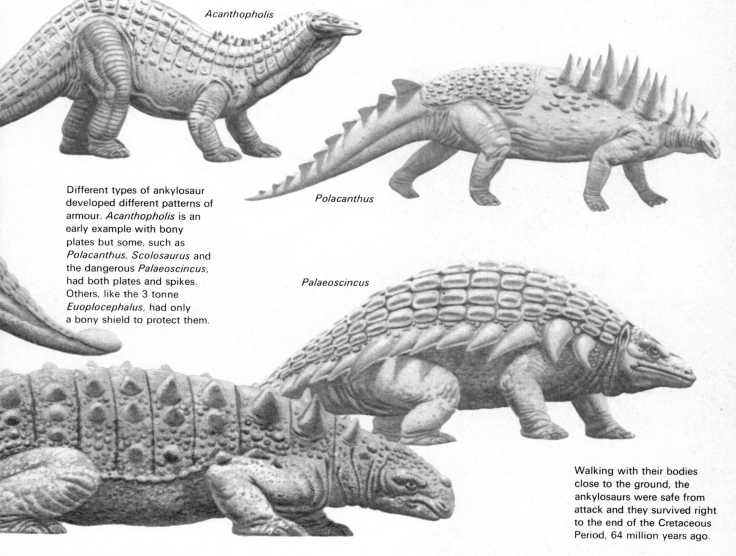

Acanthopholis

Polacanthus

Different types of ankylosaur
developed different patterns of
armour. *Acanthopholis* is an
early example with bony
plates but some, such as
Polacanthus, Scolosaurus and
the dangerous *Palaeoscincus,*
had both plates and spikes.
Others, like the 3 tonne
Euoplocephalus, had only
a bony shield to protect them.

Palaeoscincus

Walking with their bodies
close to the ground, the
ankylosaurs were safe from
attack and they survived right
to the end of the Cretaceous
Period, 64 million years ago.

Scolosaurus, another large ankylosaur weighing 3·5 tonnes, was also a very well-protected dinosaur. Its bony carapace, with its massive bony spikes, made it very difficult to attack, while the rounded bony club at the end of its tail also had two dangerous spikes. By far the most formidable ankylosaur was *Palaeoscincus*. At the edge of its armour rows of sharp spikes stuck out sideways and no enemy would have been able to approach easily.

Since these armoured dinosaurs were so difficult to attack, we would expect there to have been many of them. In fact they are quite rare and some are known from only a single specimen. One reason for this is that ankylosaurs had one weak point, the underbelly, which the side spikes developed to protect. Once on its back the ankylosaur was helpless and its bony carapace would have formed a great feeding trough full of entrails and juices, which could easily be devoured by a hungry flesh eater.

Fossil bodies of ankylosaurs are always found upside down. They could not normally have turned on their backs – they would have been much too vulnerable – but there are two possible ways in which it may have happened. If they fell into a river and drowned, they would eventually have risen to the surface belly-side uppermost. When they were finally washed up onto a sandbank they would lie upside down.

The other possibility is that some flesh eaters had learned to trap and turn them over. When the flesh had been eaten, the hard armour casing would remain untouched. This cannot have been a common event for only a few of the largest flesh eaters could have learned the trick of turning such heavy, compact animals over with their feet.

In spite of the snail's pace at which the ankylosaurs moved about, these slow, shuffling dinosaurs are found in America, Europe and Asia so they were obviously successful in their ponderous way.

IGUANODON AND THE ORNITHOPODS

One of the best known of all the dinosaurs of the Cretaceous Period was a plant-eating, bird-hipped ornithopod called *Iguanodon*. In 1822 Dr and Mrs Gideon Mantell were travelling by stage coach from London to Lewes in Sussex when, during a stop near Cuckfield, Mrs Mantell wandered off the road into the bushes. There she saw some large teeth sticking out of the rocks on the ground and brought them back for her husband to see. They were different from any teeth Dr Mantell knew and

he sent them to the world's greatest expert of the time to find out what animal they came from. The expert suggested they belonged to a rhinoceros but Dr Mantell was not satisfied with this. Then, one day when visiting a friend at the Royal College of Surgeons in London he saw some teeth belonging to a small American lizard, the *Iguana*. He realized at once that the teeth Mrs Mantell had found were gigantic versions of *Iguana* teeth and announced his discovery of an extinct giant plant-eating reptile. He named it *Iguanodon* – 'Iguana tooth'. During the next five years Mantell hunted carefully for the bones of this animal and eventually part of a skeleton was discovered.

Restorations were made from these fossil bones and were put on display at the 1851 Exhibition in

Iguanodon was a plant eater, a descendant of the bird-hipped *Camptosaurus*. Standing 5 m tall, it weighed up to 4·5 tonnes and was one of the main inhabitants of the Cretaceous lowlands. The first *Iguanodon* was found in 1822. Fifty years later a whole herd was found in an ancient ravine where they had died together 100 million years before.

London. They are still preserved in the gardens of the Crystal Palace in London. This life-size sculpture was hollow and before it was put on public show, all the fossil experts in London had a celebration dinner inside it. The model did not look at all like the real *Iguanodon*. It showed an animal with a thick, stocky body and hardly any neck at all. On the snout was a bony spike which had been found with the other bones: no-one could think of anywhere else to put it.

It was not until 1878 that anyone had enough information to show exactly what *Iguanodon* looked like. In that year coal miners at Bernissart in Belgium suddenly found themselves digging through fossil bones instead of coal. They had by chance cut their way into an ancient pit or ravine into which a herd of *Iguanodon* had fallen millions of years before. There were 31 bodies, all spread about but complete. The whole herd had perished together, larger males and smaller females, in a sudden catastrophe.

The bones were 322 m below ground, so it was an extremely difficult task to map out the individual skeletons and dig them carefully out so that they could be reassembled above ground. Some were reconstructed and put on display in the Brussels Natural History Museum, while others were laid out in exactly the same positions in which they had been found.

The skeletons proved once and for all how *Iguanodon* had looked in life. It was a two-legged animal, 5 m high and about 11 m long, weighing

up to 4·5 tonnes. It had powerful back legs and a massive tail that helped it to balance and also made a useful weapon against flesh eaters. The bony spike which had been shown on the end of its nose turned out to be the tip of its thumb and probably carried a sharp, horny claw. We still do not know exactly what this was used for but it would have been a good weapon at close quarters and could also have been used for tearing the bark of trees or for holding the female during mating.

Iguanodon's other fingers had small hooves, proving that it sometimes walked on all fours. However, most of the footprint trackways that have been found show it walking on only its back legs. The hooves on these were bigger than the front ones and we know that it walked on three toes, putting one leg in front of the other as it went.

As Mantell had realized, *Iguanodon* was a plant eater. Its teeth showed a great deal of wear and as they were worn down they were continually replaced. At the tip of its lower jaw it had the extra predentary bone, which was covered with a horny beak. Like other bird-hipped plant eaters it grasped bunches of leaves with its long tongue, then pulled them into its mouth to be clipped off with the beak and chewed up with its teeth.

Among the bird-hipped, plant-eating ornithopods of the Cretaceous Period were three unusual dinosaurs. The first, *Ouranosaurus*, was found recently in the middle of what is now the Sahara desert, its bones sticking up from the dry sand. It was first described in 1975. Though basically it was similar to *Iguanodon*, it had a row of blade-like spines down the middle of its back, forming a long, narrow sail.

Only a few other dinosaurs have been found with a sail like this. One was *Spinosaurus* and, as we have seen, its sail prevented it from overheating and helped it to warm up quickly after the cool of the night. Both the flesh-eating *Spinosaurus* and the plant-eating *Ouranosaurus* came from northern Africa and they probably lived in the same type of environment where they had to cope with the same problems. The sail gave *Spinosaurus* an important advantage over other dinosaurs. The only way for a large plant eater in the same area to avoid being caught and killed was for it to develop in the same way. With a sail of its own the plant eater could be as active as the flesh eater without overheating and so had a better chance of escaping.

The second unusual ornithopod came from North America. *Tenontosaurus* was 8 m long and weighed 1 tonne. Over half its total length was taken up by an enormous tail, measuring almost 5 m. Usually heavy tails developed to help to counterbalance the weight of the dinosaur's body when it stood on its back legs but this huge, powerful tail must have had another function as well. *Tenontosaurus* was one of the few bird-hipped plant eaters that lived in the swamps and the tail was probably specially adapted for swimming.

The bird-hipped dinosaurs developed in so many new ways during the Cretaceous Period that it is surprising to find that one of the most successful of them all was a small dinosaur that remained almost unchanged for well over 100 million years, from the beginning of the Age of Dinosaurs right through to the very end. *Hypsilophodon*, best known from the Isle of Wight in England, was only 600 mm high, 1·5 m long and weighed 67 kg. Like the very first dinosaurs the skin on its back still had a faint armour of bony plates and anyone meeting it in the Cretaceous would have had no hesitation in calling it a 'living fossil'.

When *Hypsilophodon* was first discovered, people thought that it was a tree-dweller. Its big toe seemed to be set at an angle to the other three toes, which meant that it could grasp a branch as we can with our hands. However, we now know that its four toes were parallel and that it could not possibly have perched safely.

Instead of being a tree-climber, *Hypsilophodon* was a very fast runner. Like all animals that can run swiftly, the bones of its lower leg were very long, much longer than the bones of the upper leg. Its tail was specially stiffened, particularly at the tip and it acted as an effective balancing organ so that *Hypsilophodon* could leap about, twisting and turning with agility.

Hypsilophodon was probably the fastest of all the dinosaurs and survived for so long because it was always able to outrun its enemies. When it was running its head and tail were stretched out in a straight line. When it was just wandering about looking for tender plants to eat, it held its head up like a bird's, turning it from side to side on its flexible neck.

Like all the bird-hipped dinosaurs, *Hypsilophodon* was a plant eater and it had teeth like *Iguanodon*'s, specially ridged for crushing fruits and leaves. It also had a horny beak but unlike the other ornithopods it had an upper row of small teeth at the front of its mouth. We do not know what these were used for. They do not seem to have been used for feeding for its sharp beak would have clipped off foliage effectively and did not cut against the teeth.

Ouranosaurus was a relative of Iguanodon and was found in what is now the Sahara desert. Like the flesh eater *Spinosaurus*, which lived in the same environment, it had a vertical sail down the middle of its back, supported by long spines growing from its vertebrae. Though the desert was then covered with plants and trees, the climate was hot, and *Ouranosaurus*'s sail probably prevented it from overheating.

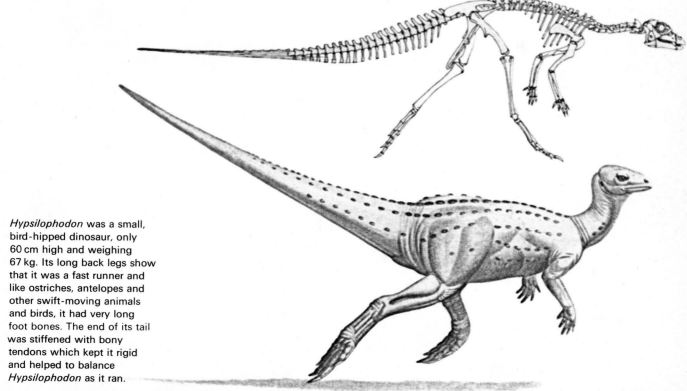

Hypsilophodon was a small, bird-hipped dinosaur, only 60 cm high and weighing 67 kg. Its long back legs show that it was a fast runner and like ostriches, antelopes and other swift-moving animals and birds, it had very long foot bones. The end of its tail was stiffened with bony tendons which kept it rigid and helped to balance *Hypsilophodon* as it ran.

THE BONE-HEADED DINOSAURS

Another group of ornithopods, the bone-headed dinosaurs, have puzzled scientists for a long time. By dinosaur standards they were small but the tops of their heads had an enormous helmet of solid bone.

The skulls which protect our own delicate brains are only about 1 cm thick yet the bone-head *Stegoceras*, which was as tall as a man, had a solid bony dome five times thicker, covering a brain only the size of a large hen's egg.

Such a strong, bony helmet must have been there for a special purpose and we can find a clue to what this was by looking at animals such as sheep and goats. These live in flocks and herds, dominated by a few powerful males. The leader of the flock is in charge of both males and females, protecting them from danger and choosing the best females for his mates. In order to become leader, however, he must prove himself by trials of strength against all the other males in the flock. The males charge each other, using their horns and heads as battering rams until at last the most powerful male subdues all his rivals. Often the male with the biggest horns will frighten the others simply with his impressive appearance. The leader stays until a younger, stronger animal defeats him.

Stegoceras may have used its head in the same way. When the males butted against one another, their heads would meet with tremendous force, but the head was attached to the backbone in such a way that the shock of impact passed down the body without causing any damage. Like rams and goats today, they would fight for the leadership of the herd and for the right to mate with the females.

The males were aggressive towards one another but they must have been very timid towards other animals for they had no real means of protecting themselves against the flesh eaters. They survived for millions of years, throughout the Cretaceous Period, in North America, Europe and Asia, because they were very agile and lived in rocky and hilly country where the giant carnosaurs could not climb to follow them.

Skeletons of bone-headed dinosaurs are very rare, for fossils are seldom found in upland areas. The solid, bony domes were, however, almost indestructible and they were often buried a long way from the place where the dinosaur had died.

The skulls were washed down from the hillside by the rains and fell eventually into a river, to be swept

The bone-headed dinosaurs, or pachycephalosaurs, were bird-hipped plant eaters, descended, like *Iguanodon* and the other ornithopods, from *Camptosaurus*. The tops of their skulls were strengthened by enormous thicknesses of solid, compact bone. In the past, scientists thought that this had been caused by a disease, the result of an overactive pituitary gland (the gland that controls growth). Recently, however, it has been suggested that they used their heads like battering rams and so needed thick skulls to protect their brains.

When the skulls are placed together, with the thickest part of one opposite the thickest part of the other, we can see that even a very forceful collision would do little harm. The skull itself would not break and the shock of the blow would pass straight down the backbone, jarring the spine but not causing any real damage.

away by the fast-flowing current. As it was dragged along on the river bed, the bone would be worn and polished like a pebble by the action of the water.

The ancestor of the bone-heads was *Yaverlandia*, a small relative of *Hypsilophodon*, from the Isle of Wight. *Yaverlandia* was about the size of a turkey and had a long, stiff tail sticking out behind. The beginnings of a bony dome are found as two patches of thickened bone, less than 1 cm thick, on top of its skull just above the eye sockets.

Much later these had developed into *Stegoceras*'s large, rounded dome with a small bony frill behind. The male dinosaurs had bigger domes, since they did the fighting, and the females had larger frills.

The giant of the bone-heads was *Pachycephalosaurus*, from Canada. Its head was three times as long as *Stegoceras*'s head and its bony dome was nearly five times as thick. It also had elaborate bony decorations on its head, sharp spikes on the end of its snout and a fringe of spiky knobs on the back of its skull.

Little more is known about the life and habits of these strange bone-headed dinosaurs but nevertheless they provide another example of the great variety of plant-eating dinosaurs that adapted successfully to life in the Cretaceous Period.

Stegoceras

Pachycephalosaurus

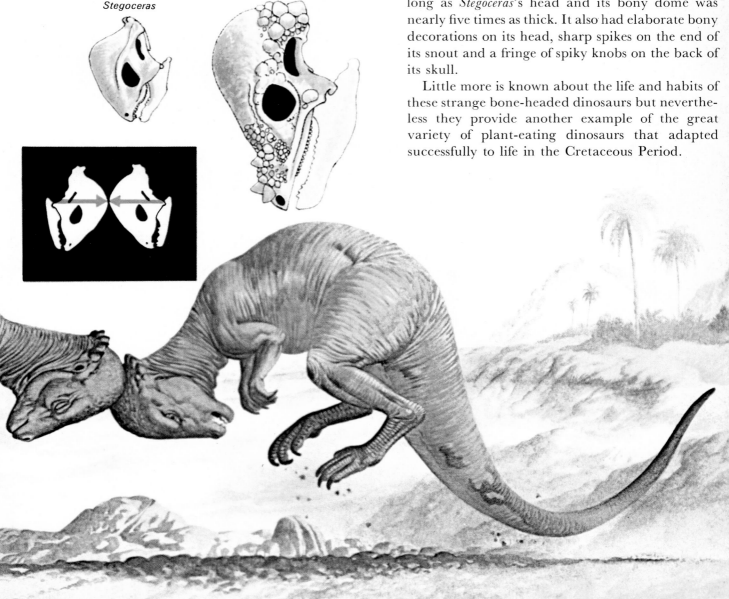

THE HADROSAURS

The duck-billed dinosaurs or hadrosaurs were by far the most successful of all the ornithopods living in the Cretaceous Period. They were descended from the bird-hipped *Camptosaurus* and looked overall very like it. They were around 9 m long and weighed about 3 tonnes. However, they developed a number of special features which distinguish them from all other dinosaurs.

Their most obvious feature, which gives them their common name, is the rounded upper jaw which was flattened at the tip and looked rather like a duck's bill. The top front edge overlapped the lower jaw and the large pointed tip of the predentary bone fitted into the bill underneath. Like all the other ornithopods they had a horny beak for pulling leaves and fruits from trees and bushes. In marshy areas they used the beak to clip off horsetail plants.

The hadrosaurs' second distinctive feature was their teeth, which evolved to deal with the new, tough flowering plants that appeared in the Cretaceous Period for the first time. Hadrosaurs had the plant eater's usual muscular cheeks and their teeth were small and ridged, tightly packed together in several rows to form a wide pavement with sharp cutting edges. As the rows of teeth in the top and bottom jaws moved across one another, the toughest plant material would be ground into minute fragments so that all the goodness could be extracted from the fibres.

The hadrosaurs' chewing action was very unusual. Small fragments of food were pushed out sideways to accumulate in the cheek pouches. The elastic cheek muscles pushed the food towards the teeth again and again until it was ground into small enough pieces. When the cheeks were full of finely-ground food, the tongue scooped it back into the main mouth cavity to be swallowed in the usual way.

The teeth were gradually worn down by the hard, woody plants but this did not matter: several new teeth grew under each one, ready to come into use when the tooth above was worn away.

The other special features of the hadrosaurs' skeleton seem to be just minor modifications to fit them for a slightly different way of life. For example we know that their hands had webbed fingers because mummified remains have been found with the dried skin preserved. Two of the four fingers were long, with small hooves on the end; the others had no hooves and were shorter. Because of the webbing between the fingers we know that hadrosaurs must have lived part of the time in the water, but the hooves tell us that they were also used to walking on land like the other ornithopods.

Like most other bird-hipped dinosaurs, a hadrosaur had back legs that were much bigger and longer than its front ones. The back feet had only three toes and these were all smaller than the toes of, for example, *Iguanodon*. The middle toe was the longest, making the foot look very like a typical bird's foot. We do not know whether the back feet were webbed like the front ones for none has so far been discovered with the skin preserved.

Hadrosaur tails were much flatter from side to side than other dinosaur tails and they were very stiff. By contrast, their necks were very mobile. All the skeletons show the tail held stiffly out in line with the back, and the flexible neck folded back on itself.

Once the basic hadrosaur skeleton had evolved in the Cretaceous Period it did not change noticeably, probably because it was already perfectly adapted for the hadrosaur's way of life. However, two bones on the front of the skull evolved into a variety of strange, complicated outgrowths which make it very easy to tell each species of hadrosaurs from all the others. As we shall see, this may have been one of their functions, for apart from their strange crests, most hadrosaurs must have looked very much alike.

The evolution of the hadrosaurs The first hadrosaur, *Batractosaurus*, comes from the early Cretaceous rocks of Mongolia. By the end of the Cretaceous, 55 million years later, we know that they were established in England, Holland, France and the Balkans in Europe; in Kazakhstan and Usbekistan; in eastern Asia from Laos in the south to the island of Sakhalin in the east and in China and Mongolia. The greatest number and variety, however, come from North America, where they evolved in several different ways. At the very end of the Cretaceous, when the land masses of North and South America were joined, they also moved into the southern continent.

An almost complete skeleton of *Batractosaurus* shows that all the basic hadrosaur features – the fingers and toes, the stiff tail and flexible neck and the rows of grinding teeth – had already developed.

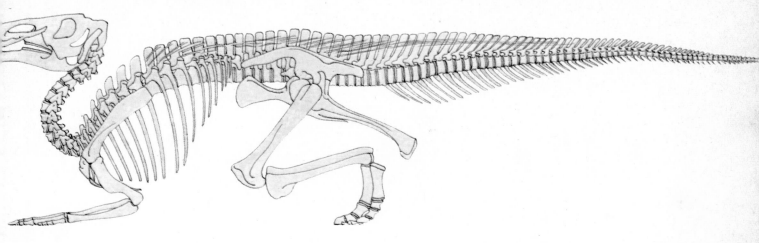

Complete skeletons of hadrosaurs are frequently found in parts of North America. *Anatosaurus* (above) is shown exactly as it was found in the rock. Hadrosaurs were about 9 m long and they had tails that were flattened from side to side, a special adaptation for swimming.

Below: Like the other hadrosaurs, *Anatosaurus* normally walked on two legs. Its tail and backbone were strengthened with bony tendons but its neck was flexible. Its front feet were webbed, another adaptation for swimming, but two of the fingers had small hooves on the end for walking. Though it weighed 3 tonnes or more, it had no difficulty in rising up from all fours, ready to run off at the slightest sign of danger.

Unfortunately the vital front part of the skull is missing so it is impossible to tell what the snout and crest looked like.

The group of hadrosaurs that changed least throughout the 40 million years of their existence is known as the flat-headed hadrosaurs. The first of these is called *Edmontosaurus* and from it several different species of a hadrosaur called *Anatosaurus* evolved. The hadrosaurs are the first group of dinosaurs where it is possible to work out the relationships of all the different types to one another and to produce a detailed family tree.

Anatosaurus species did not grow crests on the top of their skulls, but the skulls themselves developed in different ways. One, for example, had an enormously long, flat bill. Another had a bulbous swelling like a nose, giving it a rather human look.

Anatosaurus survived longer than most of the large crested hadrosaurs. We know from the fossil record that this often happens. The animals that develop in very specialized ways seem successful for a time but are often outlived by more primitive forms.

The second major group is known as the solid-crested hadrosaurs. These are descended from a close relative of the flat-headed *Edmontosaurus* called *Prosaurolophus*. *Prosaurolophus* is not itself a crested dinosaur, though the bones of its skull show the beginnings of a crest. The first real solid-crested dinosaur is *Saurolophus*, one of the very few hadrosaurs found both in Asia (in Mongolia) and in North America.

All the hadrosaurs' bony crests were made from greatly lengthened premaxilla and nasal or nose bones. In *Saurolophus* both these bones project beyond the back of the skull, forming a solid spike of bone. In the Mongolian species the spike follows the line of the snout, but in the American one it curves upwards slightly.

Two solid-crested hadrosaurs, *Tsintaosaurus* from China and *Brachylophosaurus* from Canada, show the extreme developments of dinosaurs in this group. *Tsintaosaurus* had a long spike which was turned forwards until it made a useful weapon. *Brachylophosaurus*, on the other hand, had only a minute spike on the top of its head, so small that it was almost invisible.

The third group to develop was the hollow-crested hadrosaurs. The first of these were *Procheneosaurus* and *Cheneosaurus*, the smallest of all the hadrosaurs with skulls only 30 cm long instead of the normal 90 cm. Their crests jutted out above and sometimes between the eyes. The main difference between these and the earlier hadrosaurs is that their crests were hollow. There were several different species of *Procheneosaurus* and they can easily be recognized by the different shapes of their crests.

The larger hollow-crested hadrosaurs evolved the most extraordinary head decorations. *Corythosaurus* had a semi-circular ridge running along the midline of its head, doubling the height of the skull and projecting behind it, sometimes with a bony spike on the end. Again, each species had a different shaped crest: some were symmetrical, while others had irregularly shaped tops.

Lambeosaurus was similar to *Corythosaurus*. Its crest projected forwards at eye level and always had a solid bony spike at the back end. One of its species, *Lambeosaurus magnicristatus* or 'great crested' had a crest that was larger than the whole of the rest of its skull together.

The most dramatic-looking crest of all belonged to *Parasaurolophus*. It projected well behind the skull, then folded back to reach just above the eyes. Sometimes the crest projected as much as one and a half times the length of the skull and in one specimen the distance from the tip of the snout to the end of the crest is 2 m.

The fact that so many species developed hollow crests means that they must have given the hadrosaurs some advantages in the struggle for survival. Not surprisingly, there have been many arguments about the real purpose of these strange nose extensions and it is only recently that scientists have solved the problem satisfactorily.

Hadrosaur heads One of the most popular theories about the hollow crests is that they enabled the hadrosaurs to store air when they were under water, rather like a diver's oxygen cylinder. It is difficult to imagine how this could have worked, for the crests could not have held very much air at a time, certainly not enough to fill the lungs. No other air-breathing water animal has developed similar head decorations for this purpose, so it seems more likely that there was some other reason for them.

The skulls of many of the hollow-crested hadrosaurs are so well preserved that minute details of their internal structure can be studied. From them we can see that the crests were not just hollow bones full of air, but were filled with complicated nasal passages. In the earliest hollow-crested hadrosaur, *Procheneosaurus*, the nasal passages reach as far as the eyes, then bend forwards to enter the

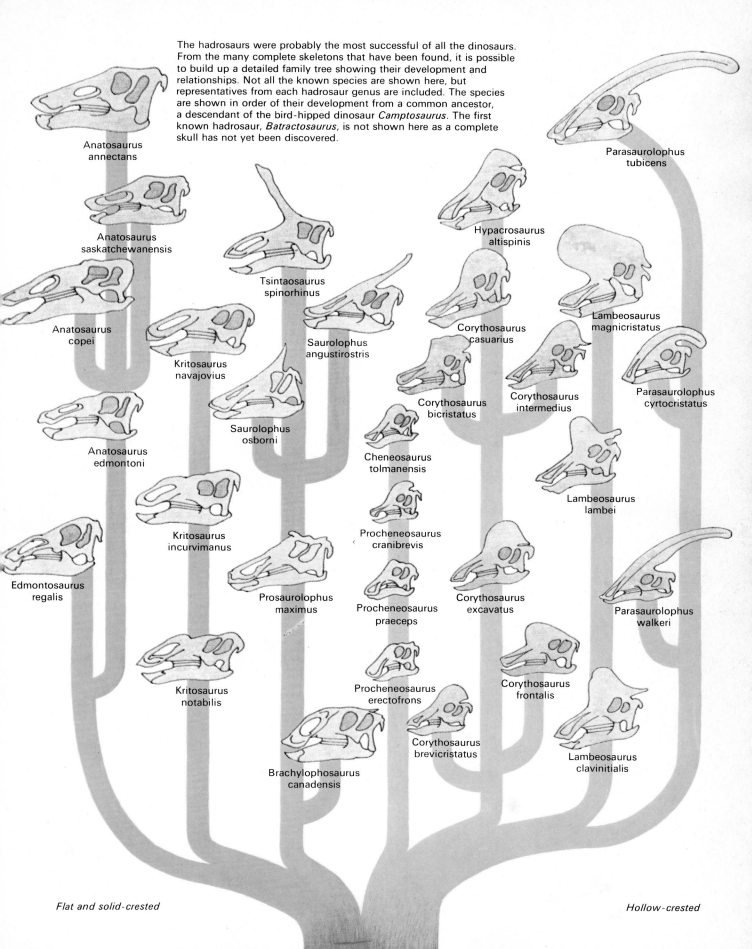

The hadrosaurs were probably the most successful of all the dinosaurs. From the many complete skeletons that have been found, it is possible to build up a detailed family tree showing their development and relationships. Not all the known species are shown here, but representatives from each hadrosaur genus are included. The species are shown in order of their development from a common ancestor, a descendant of the bird-hipped dinosaur *Camptosaurus*. The first known hadrosaur, *Batractosaurus*, is not shown here as a complete skull has not yet been discovered.

Anatosaurus
annectans

Parasaurolophus
tubicens

Anatosaurus
saskatchewanensis

Tsintaosaurus
spinorhinus

Hypacrosaurus
altispinis

Anatosaurus
copei

Saurolophus
angustirostris

Corythosaurus
casuarius

Lambeosaurus
magnicristatus

Kritosaurus
navajovius

Corythosaurus
bicristatus

Corythosaurus
intermedius

Parasaurolophus
cyrtocristatus

Saurolophus
osborni

Anatosaurus
edmontoni

Cheneosaurus
tolmanensis

Kritosaurus
incurvimanus

Lambeosaurus
lambei

Procheneosaurus
cranibrevis

Edmontosaurus
regalis

Prosaurolophus
maximus

Procheneosaurus
praeceps

Corythosaurus
excavatus

Parasaurolophus
walkeri

Kritosaurus
notabilis

Procheneosaurus
erectofrons

Corythosaurus
frontalis

Corythosaurus
brevicristatus

Lambeosaurus
clavinitialis

Brachylophosaurus
canadensis

Flat and solid-crested

Hollow-crested

93

main cavity of the crest. Twisting and turning they eventually link up with the windpipe leading down to the lungs. As the crests become more complicated, so does the route of the nasal passages, which sometimes extends right to the tip of the crest before running back again to the top of the skull.

The nasal passages would have been lined with soft tissues which have not, of course, been preserved. Today mammals use the soft tissues in their nose to clean and filter the air and to make it warm and humid before it goes to the lungs. Some sand-living lizards have nasal passages that point upwards like a hadrosaur's before leading down to the windpipe. These help to prevent sand from getting to the lungs. Hadrosaurs probably did not bury their head in the sand, but they may well have been troubled by pollen from the flowering plants, scattered in the air when they pulled off the leaves and flower heads.

It is most unlikely that the hadrosaurs developed their complicated crests just to avoid hayfever. It is much more probable that they were connected with the sense of smell. The soft tissues contained special smelling membranes and because the nasal passages were so long and complicated, there was more soft tissue surface than usual. The sense of smell would therefore have been greatly improved.

The shape of hadrosaur brains seems to prove that this theory is correct. Casts of hollowed-out brain-cases show the shape of the brain, the places where the different nerves entered and left, and the sizes of the different areas of the brain. Casts of hollow-crested hadrosaur brain-cases show that the part of the brain used for smelling probably fitted into the floor of the crest cavity. Because the network of nerves here was in close contact with the sensitive smelling membrane of the nasal passages, the hadrosaur's sense of smell would have been particularly acute.

The crests probably also acted as recognition signals between members of the same hadrosaur species. Today many animals that look rather alike use signals in the same way. Many kinds of gulls, for example, have differently coloured rings round their eyes to help them choose a mate of the right species, and also to help the young to identify their parents.

If the crests were to be useful in this way, hadrosaurs would have needed good eyesight. We know from the skeleton's eye sockets that this was in fact the case. Hadrosaurs had eyes about 100 mm across, giving them wide-angle vision, and a large,

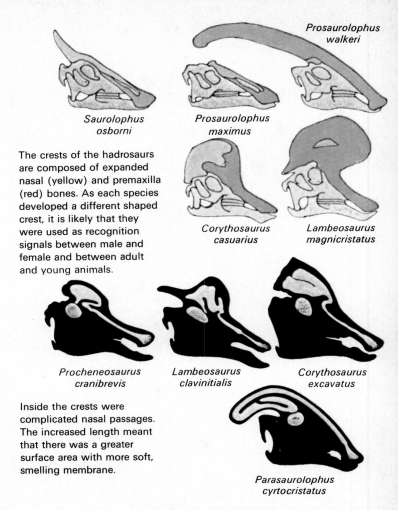

Prosaurolophus walkeri

Saurolophus osborni

Prosaurolophus maximus

The crests of the hadrosaurs are composed of expanded nasal (yellow) and premaxilla (red) bones. As each species developed a different shaped crest, it is likely that they were used as recognition signals between male and female and between adult and young animals.

Corythosaurus casuarius

Lambeosaurus magnicristatus

Procheneosaurus cranibrevis

Lambeosaurus clavinitialis

Corythosaurus excavatus

Inside the crests were complicated nasal passages. The increased length meant that there was a greater surface area with more soft, smelling membrane.

Parasaurolophus cyrtocristatus

efficient optic nerve, a further sign of good eyesight.

Hadrosaurs therefore had good sight and a good sense of smell. For a long time no-one knew whether they – or any other dinosaurs – could hear or not. This was because the bones of the middle ear which conduct sound were very delicate and were not normally preserved with the rest of the skull. However, a skull belonging to the hadrosaur *Corythosaurus* has now been found with the fragile hearing bone intact. *Corythosaurus* was a large animal, 9 m long, but the sound-conducting bone was extremely fine, only 50 mm long and 2·5 mm thick at its thickest end. Such a delicate bone would have been very sensitive to vibrations and it proves that hadrosaurs could hear well.

We do not know whether hadrosaurs could make sounds. The only living reptiles that can do this are crocodiles, which are very noisy in the mating season. Crocodiles belong to the same order as dinosaurs – the archosaurs – and though they have survived into our own time, they are more primitive than the dinosaurs. Hadrosaurs were much more advanced reptiles, and would surely not have lost the ability to communicate with one another by sound.

There is no way of knowing exactly what kind

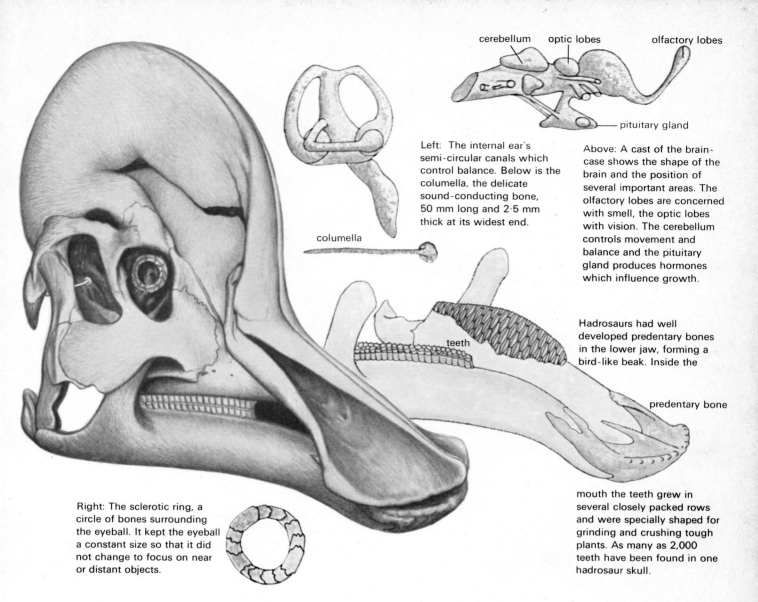

cerebellum optic lobes olfactory lobes

pituitary gland

Left: The internal ear's semi-circular canals which control balance. Below is the columella, the delicate sound-conducting bone, 50 mm long and 2·5 mm thick at its widest end.

columella

Above: A cast of the brain-case shows the shape of the brain and the position of several important areas. The olfactory lobes are concerned with smell, the optic lobes with vision. The cerebellum controls movement and balance and the pituitary gland produces hormones which influence growth.

Hadrosaurs had well developed predentary bones in the lower jaw, forming a bird-like beak. Inside the

teeth

predentary bone

Right: The sclerotic ring, a circle of bones surrounding the eyeball. It kept the eyeball a constant size so that it did not change to focus on near or distant objects.

mouth the teeth grew in several closely packed rows and were specially shaped for grinding and crushing tough plants. As many as 2,000 teeth have been found in one hadrosaur skull.

of noises they made but it is fairly certain that they were not silent animals. Wherever they went, the air would have been filled with the sound of bellowing and grunting dinosaurs.

How the hadrosaurs lived There were more species of hadrosaur and more animals of each species than any other dinosaurs at the end of the Cretaceous. Yet it is difficult to see just why they were so successful. They seem to have been the most defenceless of all the dinosaurs and had no possible way of protecting themselves from attack. They were too heavy to run fast and they had no sharp claws or talons, and no spiky armour like the ankylosaurs. Their acute sense of smell may have helped them here: with the wind in the right direction they could sense predators approaching from far away and escape into the water.

Much of the evidence we have about the way they lived seems to be contradictory. Their skeletons were adapted for life in the water. The deep,

narrow tail was an ideal swimming organ and webbed feet would have been of no use to an animal living entirely on land. Their teeth, however, were adapted for feeding on land plants that needed grinding and crushing. If they had eaten mainly soft water weeds, their highly developed jaws and teeth would not have been necessary.

The fossilized contents of their stomachs prove without doubt that they ate land plants. Pine needles, pieces of twigs and the remains of seeds and fruits have all been found, proving that hadrosaurs could and did feed on the toughest modern land plants. Many of the complete skeletons found are mummified, which could only have happened in dry conditions: and the rocks in which they are found seem to have been formed on open plains rather than in swamps and marshes. Ninety-five per cent of fossil plants in the same rocks are land plants, and only 5 per cent are from the water.

Perhaps the hadrosaurs were swamp dwellers,

coming occasionally to drier land to feed. This would explain why there are no semi-aquatic sauropods in regions where the hadrosaurs flourished. Some scientists argue that hadrosaurs only developed their swimming tails and webbed feet to help them to escape from predators, and that they spent most of their time on land. But it is unlikely that such major changes to the animal's skeleton would have evolved simply to allow them to escape if water happened to be nearby when they were attacked.

The only explanation that seems to fit all the contradictory evidence is that they lived in the water when they were young, and moved onto dry land later on. The mother dinosaur laid her eggs near the water and, when they hatched, the young made their way to the safety of the swamps and marshes. They spent some years swimming there,

secure from the dangerous flesh-eating dinosaurs of the land. Their swimming tail and webbed feet helped them to move well in the water, and they were able to feed on the soft water plants.

As they grew older they ventured further from the water, feeding on tougher and tougher plant material which their teeth were now adapted to cope with. The swimming tail acted as an effective counterbalance when they stood on their back legs to reach the branches of trees, and the webbed hands were no more than a reminder of their earlier, swamp-living days. The small hooves on the fingers and toes made it possible for them to walk easily on land.

To support this argument, no young hadrosaur skeletons have ever been found in the same place as the adults, so it seems almost certain that they grew up in a different environment.

Parasaurolophus's great hollow crest was 2 m from snout to tip. Like other hadrosaurs, adults probably lived on land, feeding on pines and other tough branches, while the young grew up in the swamps, using their swimming tails and webbed fingers to propel them through the water.

THE CERATOPSIANS

The last group of dinosaurs to develop was the horned and frilled dinosaurs, the ceratopsians. They are known as horned and frilled because the bones at the back of the skull grew into an enormous frill, which extended over the back of the neck. Above the eyes and on the snout the frills carried large, sharp horns.

The ancestors of the ceratopsians were plant-eating ornithopods from Mongolia. The best known is *Psittacosaurus* or 'parrot reptile', named because it had a hooked beak like a parrot's. *Psittacosaurus* does not look at all like a ceratopsian but the faintest hint of a bony frill at the back of its skull shows that it was probably the forerunner of the true frilled dinosaurs.

Psittacosaurus was a small animal, only 2 m long. When compared with the light, bouncy *Hypsilophodon*, which was about the same length, it seems rather heavily built for its size. From its general proportions we can tell that it usually walked about on its hind feet like most other ornithopods. However, its sturdy front legs do not look capable of grasping and they, too, were used for walking. *Psittacosaurus* is especially significant because it shows a half-way stage between the typical two-legged ornithopods and the new four-legged ceratopsians: *Psittacosaurus* itself could walk equally well on two legs or on four.

One of the problems with *Psittacosaurus* is how it managed not only to survive but to evolve into many new forms. It was small but slow moving and it did not have any way of defending itself. The bony frill that later grew on the skulls of its descendants did not develop for protection but for a quite different purpose.

At the beginning of the Cretaceous Period, the dinosaurs faced a serious crisis in their food supply. *Psittacosaurus* shows how they were beginning to deal with the changes in plant life. New, tougher plants were replacing the soft ferns and rushes that had grown during the Jurassic and, in order to survive, the dinosaurs had to adapt to them. First,

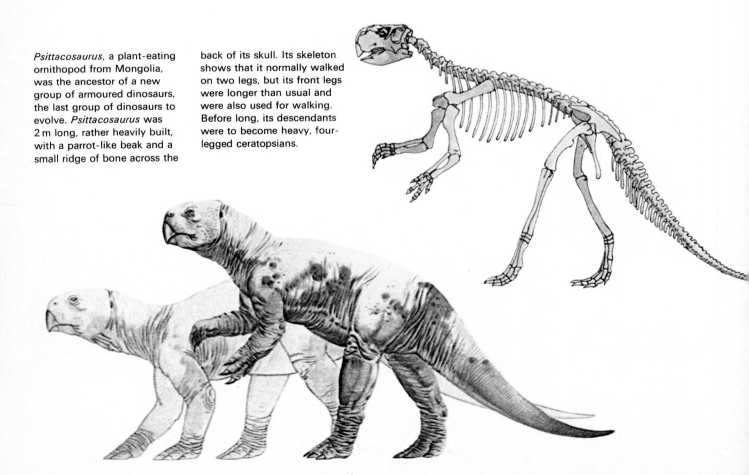

Psittacosaurus, a plant-eating ornithopod from Mongolia, was the ancestor of a new group of armoured dinosaurs, the last group of dinosaurs to evolve. *Psittacosaurus* was 2 m long, rather heavily built, with a parrot-like beak and a small ridge of bone across the back of its skull. Its skeleton shows that it normally walked on two legs, but its front legs were longer than usual and were also used for walking. Before long, its descendants were to become heavy, four-legged ceratopsians.

a sharper cutting beak was formed and more jaw muscles developed to strengthen the jaws for tugging and biting.

In the first true, frilled dinosaur, *Protoceratops*, these developments have been carried further. Known only from Mongolia, *Protoceratops* is the direct ancestor of all the later ceratopsians and had already begun to look like them in many ways. Like *Psittacosaurus* it was about 2 m long, but it had a shorter tail and its head was large in proportion to its body. It had completely lost the ability to walk upright on its back legs. All its legs had become shorter and it was altogether a much more squat animal, weighing over 1·5 tonnes, though it was only 75 cm high at the hip.

Its cropping beak was much stronger and was also narrower and sharper. Its teeth had become longer and sharper to deal with the tougher plants it had to eat. A proper bony frill had developed at the back of its skull.

When the skull is studied, the frill looks as though it was there principally to protect the vulnerable neck. In fact it bulged with massive jaw muscles which gave it a very powerful bite, but did not provide any kind of protection. *Protoceratops* was even more vulnerable than *Psittacosaurus* yet it continued to flourish. We know that it fed on very tough plants and it must have discovered a new source of food in areas where it was safe from the attentions of the flesh-eating dinosaurs.

Protoceratops did not eat leaves and fruit, for its teeth were adapted for slicing not crushing, and although modern plants had appeared, its sharp beak and shearing teeth were not suitable for dealing with them. What then did it eat?

In the later part of the Cretaceous, palm trees had become common. Their big, leafy fronds were exceptionally fibrous and tough and only an animal with very powerful cutting teeth and jaws could chop them into small enough pieces. The ceratopsians were the first dinosaurs to be able to deal with this plant food, which was much tougher even than the horsetails that the other ornithopods had learned to eat.

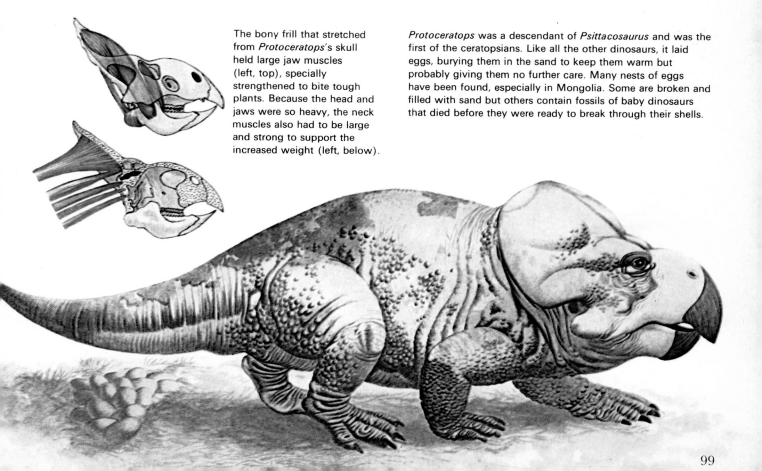

The bony frill that stretched from *Protoceratops*'s skull held large jaw muscles (left, top), specially strengthened to bite tough plants. Because the head and jaws were so heavy, the neck muscles also had to be large and strong to support the increased weight (left, below).

Protoceratops was a descendant of *Psittacosaurus* and was the first of the ceratopsians. Like all the other dinosaurs, it laid eggs, burying them in the sand to keep them warm but probably giving them no further care. Many nests of eggs have been found, especially in Mongolia. Some are broken and filled with sand but others contain fossils of baby dinosaurs that died before they were ready to break through their shells.

The palms provided a relatively safe environment for *Protoceratops*. They grew in groves, with their trunks close together and great fronds radiating out from the tops. The trees were not very tall and because the fronds were spiky, only small, stocky animals like *Protoceratops* could venture in without being scratched and wounded. Larger, more active hunters avoided the area.

The sap of the palm is a very sweet, nourishing juice and it probably formed *Protoceratops's* main food. As it chopped up the fronds, the milky sap would run out into its mouth. Today in tropical countries palm sap is tapped by man and drunk as palm wine. The ceratopsians were the very first palm wine drinkers.

The evolution of the ceratopsians The greatest variety of different ceratopsians is found in North America, where around eighteen different kinds of these frilled dinosaurs lived. From the small *Protoceratops* much larger forms evolved, some over three times its size and weighing 8·5 tonnes, five times as much as their Mongolian ancestor. As they became gradually larger and larger their tails became proportionately shorter. *Protoceratops's* head was very large compared to the size of its body. As its descendants evolved they formed two major groups: the short-frilled dinosaurs with larger and larger heads and the long-frilled dinosaurs with relatively smaller and smaller ones.

As the ceratopsians grew larger they began to develop bony outgrowths on the top of their skulls. Some of these were over a metre long and must, like the horns of the rhinoceros, have been very effective weapons against large flesh eaters. Some ceratopsians had long spikes growing as single horns on the snout. Others had double horns over the eyes and others again had large, sharp projections on the back edge of the bony frill. As the ceratopsians grew larger, so too did their horns.

All the ceratopsians, whatever kind of horn they carried, developed narrower and narrower horny beaks with a neat row of teeth giving a very sharp cutting edge. The upper and lower teeth worked

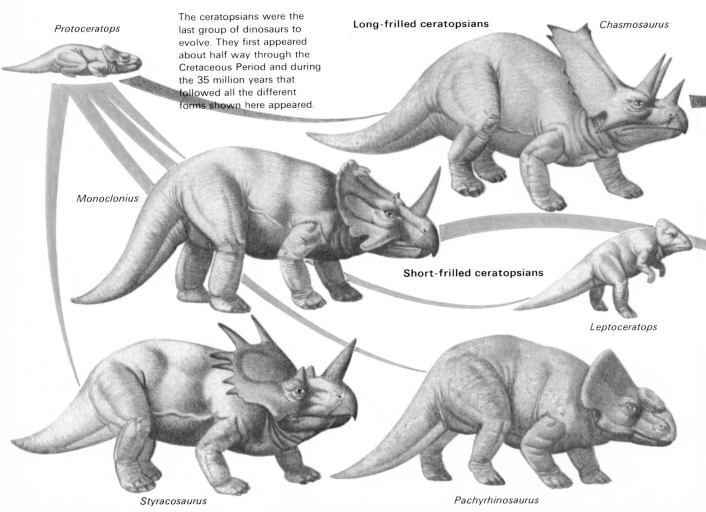

Protoceratops

The ceratopsians were the last group of dinosaurs to evolve. They first appeared about half way through the Cretaceous Period and during the 35 million years that followed all the different forms shown here appeared.

Long-frilled ceratopsians

Chasmosaurus

Monoclonius

Short-frilled ceratopsians

Leptoceratops

Styracosaurus

Pachyrhinosaurus

like a pair of scissors and could chop up the very toughest plant material. The rows of teeth grew longer so that the cutting edge was lengthened and their bite grew even more powerful than before.

The arrangement of the jaw muscles in the bony frill was different in the two groups but the actual force of the bite would have been much the same. They were both equally good at cutting up palms to get at the palm wine.

One of the first short-frilled ceratopsians to develop horns was *Monoclonius* which had a large spike on its snout and small knobs above its eye sockets. *Styracosaurus*, which lived at the same time, also had one horn on its nose but the back edge of its frill grew into an elaborate and dramatic series of spikes. The greatest and best known of the ceratopsians is *Triceratops*. Eleven metres long, weighing 8.5 tonnes, it lumbered along on its four legs. It had three horns, one on its snout and two over its eyes. As the horns could be up to a metre long, they must have been dangerous weapons against any enemy.

One odd member of the short-frilled group, *Pachyrhinosaurus*, did not develop spikes or horns. Instead a thick, bony lump formed on the top of its head between its eyes.

The long-frilled group grew horns over their eyes but their snout horns never became very large. Their main feature was a very long frill which grew until it covered most of the animal's back as protective armour plating. *Torosaurus*, the largest of the long-frilled group, had a skull which was nearly 3 m long, covering its back like a bony blanket.

With all the horned dinosaurs doing so well, it is surprising to find one ceratopsian which developed in a quite different way. Instead of growing a bony frill and stocky body like all its relatives, it had no frill at all and its skeleton was light and slender. *Leptoceratops* was 2 m long and weighed only 55 kg; instead of being a ponderous palm eater it became a fast, agile runner. Only its skull and teeth prove that it belonged to the same group as the great *Triceratops*.

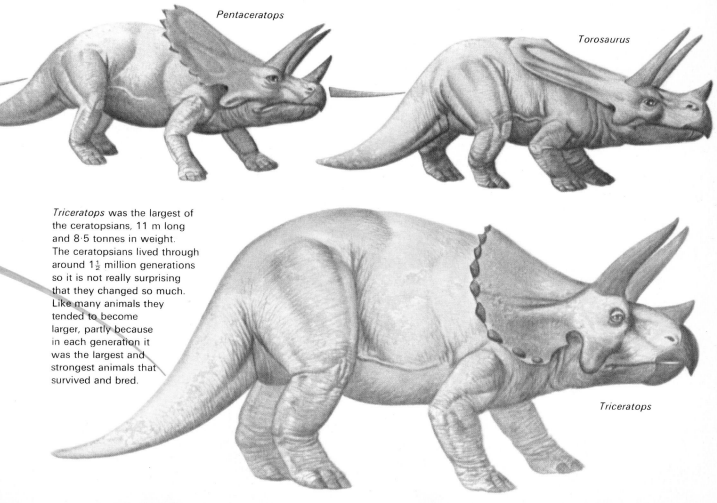

Pentaceratops

Torosaurus

Triceratops was the largest of the ceratopsians, 11 m long and 8.5 tonnes in weight. The ceratopsians lived through around $1\frac{1}{2}$ million generations so it is not really surprising that they changed so much. Like many animals they tended to become larger, partly because in each generation it was the largest and strongest animals that survived and bred.

Triceratops

EARLY CRETACEOUS LOWLANDS

In the early part of the Cretaceous there was little to show that sweeping changes were soon to follow in both the animal and the plant life. One region where the details of the environment have been carefully studied is the south-east of England, and a very accurate picture can be built up of the way the area must have looked 120 million years ago.

At the edge of the region were mountains, forming part of a block, the London Platform, that had been pushed up by earth movements. Now the London Platform has been completely buried by newer rocks but then the mountains looked very like the steep walls of the Great Rift Valley in East Africa. The summit of the highlands was covered by cloud and as there was a monsoon climate, with dry and wet seasons, heavy, continuous downpours fell for a large part of the year.

At the foot of the mountain range the lower slopes were thickly forested with conifers, monkey puzzle trees, cycads and ferns – all plants that were familiar from the earlier Jurassic Period. A large number of different dinosaurs lived in this part of the country. The first of the bone-headed dinosaurs, *Yaverlandia*, is found here and the earliest known

Ornithodesmus

Polacanthus

Hypsilophodon

Megalosaurus

examples of two armoured ankylosaur groups, *Acanthopholis* and *Hylaeosaurus*. Groups of small, agile *Hypsilophodon* were common. Among the flesh eaters were *Megalosaurus* and *Altispinax*, the first flesh eater with a fin on its back. It must have been a good area for dinosaurs, for several new types evolved here early in the Cretaceous.

The foothills of the London mountains provided a very varied environment, with trees and shrubs and fast-flowing rivers. In marked contrast was a vast, flat-monotonous plain known as Pallenland, which extended from south-east England to France and Belgium. Pallenland covered thousands of square kilometres, all looking very much the same, with meadows of *Equisetites*, horsetails or scouring rushes. Hundreds of small streams crossed the plain, meandering across the flat land, dividing and rejoining one another to provide a dense network of waterways.

There was little rain in Pallenland, but the streams were kept full by rain from the neighbouring mountain ranges and there were seasonal floods across the entire area.

During the drier season of the year some of the streams dried up to leave just a string of isolated ponds. Living in the waters were fishes and crocodiles while in the sky were large fish-eating pterosaurs, such as *Ornithodesmus*.

Apart from these, the only obvious signs of life were the herds of *Iguanodon* grazing on the rushes. The horsetails wore teeth down rapidly and the rocks of Pallenland contain thousands of worn down *Iguanodon* teeth.

Sometimes during particularly violent floods an *Iguanodon* was swept down a channel and drowned. When the waters receded it was left partly sinking into the soft mud. One *Iguanodon* found like this has fossils of fast-growing horsetails poking up through its skeleton. In a nearby stream another *Iguanodon* has left a remarkable record of its skin pattern, pressed into the ground as it sat down on the damp ground beside a pool of water to drink.

136 million years ago much of Europe was a vast, flat plain, criss-crossed by a network of small rivers. The foothills of the London mountains provided a more varied environment, with trees and shrubs and a number of different kinds of dinosaurs.

Iguanodon

Goniopholis

Freshwater turtles

LATE CRETACEOUS LOWLANDS

The second part of the Cretaceous Period, which began about 100 million years ago, contrasts dramatically with the early part, mainly because the plant life had become quite modern. The landscape was mostly woodland, with oak trees, poplars, horse chestnuts, sycamores, maples, birch, ash and such modern tropical trees as the breadfruit, fig and palm. The plants that had been characteristic of the Jurassic Period, the conifers such as *Araucites* and the sequoia and ginkgo were still there but they were overshadowed by the newly evolved plants.

Dinosaurs look quite incongruous in such familiar woodland surroundings. Some of the giant sauropods were still there – the last one to remain in North America is named *Alamosaurus*. The great flesh eater *Tyrannosaurus* also survived until the very end of the Cretaceous. Among the small, light coelurosaurs, the last were *Ornithomimus* and its relatives, which had lost their teeth and changed from a purely meat diet to become mixed feeders, eating eggs, insects, small lizards and plants.

The two groups of lizard-hipped saurischian dinosaurs – the plant-eating sauropods and the flesh eating theropods (carnosaurs and coeluro-

Torosaurus

Triceratops

Ornithomimus

Some giant flesh- and plant-eating dinosaurs survived right to the end of the Cretaceous Period, apparently adapting successfully to the new plant life around them. Bird-hipped plant eaters flourished and there was no sign that the great dinosaurs were soon to become extinct.

Alamosaurus

Tyrannosaurus

saurs) – still flourished but they formed only a small proportion of the dinosaurs living in the late Cretaceous. The dominant dinosaurs of the time were the bird-hipped ornithischians – the ankylosaurs, the ceratopsians and, above all the duck-billed hadrosaurs. All these were apparently flourishing and increasing: there was still no sign that they were shortly to face extinction.

CRETACEOUS MARINE REPTILES

Towards the end of the Cretaceous Period, there were large areas of warm, clear, shallow seas. In these, shoals of fast, modern, bony fishes swam. In the skies above were flocks of fast-flying birds, *Ichthyornis*, which frequently dived down into the water to snatch a fish. Several kinds of flightless, toothed birds swam on the surface, also diving down beneath the water now and again to feed. Giant marine turtles called *Archelon* swam in surface waters. Though they were 4 m long, larger than any living turtles, they were not basically different from the leathery and green turtles found in today's warm oceans.

On land, the Cretaceous brought fundamental changes to both the plants and the animals but in the sea, developments were not so obvious or so dramatic. The new kinds of fish provided a new food source for any predator agile enough to catch them but most of the familiar food-animals such as the cephalopods and shellfish survived. The ichthyosaurs vanished before the end of the Cretaceous and the pliosaurs only survived in the waters around New Zealand. These had seemed the two animals most effectively adapted for life as marine predators and we do not know why they disappeared at this time.

Ammonites were shelled relatives of squids and cuttlefish. The shells which protected the animals inside were very hard. This one, with holes punched by the teeth of a young mosasaur, was bitten sixteen times.

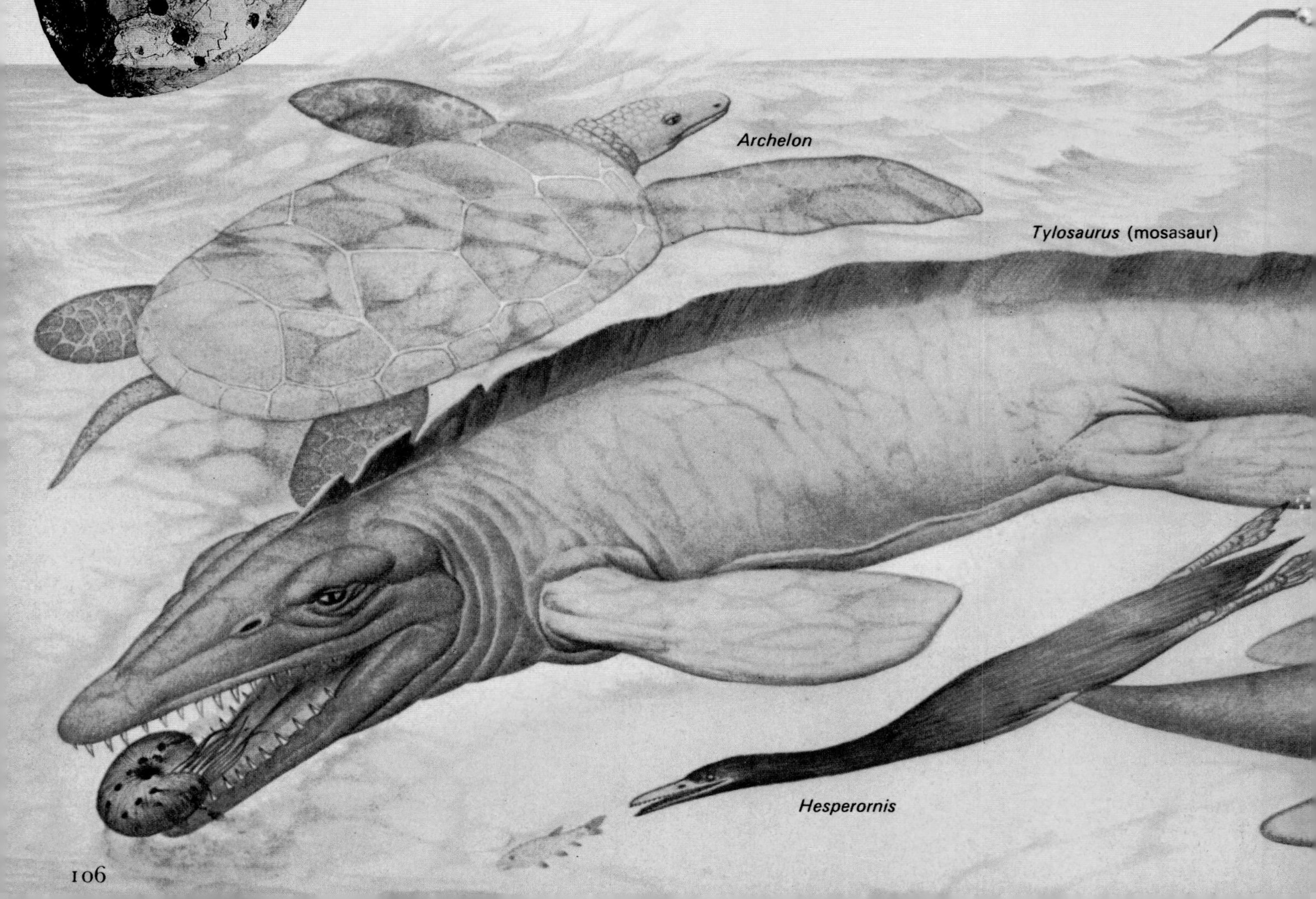

Archelon

Tylosaurus (mosasaur)

Hesperornis

The long-necked plesiosaurs now became the dominant reptiles of the sea, with a group of swimming lizards called mosasaurs. The plesiosaurs evolved into elasmosaurs, growing even longer necks, specially adapted for darting onto the fast-swimming fishes. They also produced a group called cimoliasaurs. These had large heads and short necks, looking overall rather like the streamlined pliosaurs which had by now almost completely vanished from the sea.

The swimming lizards, the mosasaurs, had long, serpentine bodies. Their long tail was flattened from side to side to drive them through the water and their limbs formed short, rounded paddles which they used for steering.

Mosasaurs had large, conical teeth, all fairly well spaced out in their jaws. These show that they were cephalopod eaters as the ichthyosaurs and pliosaurs had been. The cephalopods they fed on had hard shells and strong teeth were needed to

Ichthyornis

Hydrotherosaurus (plesiosaur)

Reptiles did not develop as dramatically in the sea as on land during the Cretaceous Period, though there were new kinds of fish and new fast-flying birds. The long-necked plesiosaurs became dominant, with the mosasaurs. The giant marine turtles that swam near the surface were larger, but not very different from today's green and leathery turtles.

crack them and reach the animal that lived inside.

A few years ago an ammonite shell was found perforated by many large holes. The shell was 260 mm across and had obviously been bitten by a toothed animal of some kind. The size of the tooth marks and their spacing fits exactly the tooth pattern of a young mosasaur. Apparently the young, inexperienced animal had tackled a cephalopod that was a little too large for it and had had to bite it sixteen times before it managed to kill it.

The very last of the mosasaurs was *Globidens*, which lived for only a few million years at the very end of the Cretaceous. Instead of eating cephalopods it lived on shellfish such as oysters and clams as the placodonts had done in the Triassic and as the walrus does today.

THE GREAT GLIDERS

Soaring over the Cretaceous oceans were giant furry pterosaurs with leathery wings, the last of the long line of flying 'reptiles' that had evolved 70 million years before. The skeleton of one of these, *Pteranodon*, was first described in 1910 but it was not until 1974 that a real study was made of its flight.

Pteranodon had a wingspan of 6·95 m, nearly as wide as a football goal mouth. This is double the span of the largest flying birds known today. The length of one wing from shoulder joint to wing tip was 3·29 m while the total span of an ocean-going albatross is rarely more than 3 m.

Overall, *Pteranodon* was 279 cm long. Its large head accounted for 179 cm of this, its neck and body making up the other 100 cm. On its head it had an enormous crest of bone, 68 cm long but only 3 mm thick, projecting from the back of its skull. In spite of *Pteranodon*'s large size, the walls of its hollow bones were never more than 5 mm thick. The skeleton must have been very fragile and it is amazing that such a delicate animal managed to fly and, even more important, to land, without smashing itself to pieces.

From calculations of its weight and the area of its wings we know that *Pteranodon* was primarily a glider, floating on the air currents rising off the waves and the cliff faces where it roosted. In most places *Pteranodon* would have needed to do little more than stretch out its wings to become airborne though it would probably not have been able to take off in still air or from a flat surface. Calculations also show that it could propel itself through the air, a single flap of its great wings taking a full two seconds.

Perhaps the most striking and unusual feature about *Pteranodon* is its long, bony crest. At first sight this seems to add extra weight – something which most flying animals avoid at all costs. Tests in wind tunnels have proved that the crest acted as a balance when *Pteranodon* turned its head far round to the side – it could turn more than half way round on its neck. The crest weighed only 30 gm because the bone it was made of was so thin. If it had not been there to provide balance, *Pteranodon* would have needed vast neck muscles weighing as much as 200 gm to do the same job. So in fact the heavy-looking crest was there to reduce weight rather than to increase it.

Pteranodon caught its food in its long beak, not with the talons of its back legs. A heavy fish carried in its feet would have upset its delicate balance, but in its beak or in the pouch at its throat, the extra weight would have had only a slight effect.

Scientists have always thought that *Pteranodon* was the largest possible flying animal but early in 1975 the discovery of a new, even larger pterosaur was announced. Its wingspan has been estimated at 15 m, nearly twice as wide as a goal mouth and bigger than a small plane. If we make the same kind of calculations that aeronautical engineers make to test the design of a new aeroplane, it seems that the greatest possible wingspan would be not 15 m but 10 m. Even so, it would have been an enormous and impressive animal.

Only isolated fragments of bone have so far been found, but from these it is possible to work out that the upper arm bone was twice as long as *Pteranodon*'s, the back legs twice as long and some of the neck bones seven times as long. We also know that it had no crest and a long beak.

Unlike *Pteranodon*, this new pterosaur was found far inland. It probably lived as vultures do on the plains of Africa and India, soaring high in the air and swooping down to eat dead animals on the ground. Compared to the size of its body, its wings were shorter than *Pteranodon*'s. Like vultures, which also have comparatively short wings, it would have been able to use the rising bubbles of hot air (thermals) which occur over the land. We shall have to wait for the full scientific details to be published before we know whether this interpretation is correct, but the giant pterosaur has already been named *Quetzalcoatlus*.

The giant gliding and soaring pterosaurs were the last of the flying 'reptiles': as they disappeared, true modern birds established themselves firmly on the coasts, on the edges of rivers and lakes, in the forests and on the plains.

Pteranodon was a large, ocean-going pterosaur, one of the last descendants of the furry flying reptiles that evolved during the Triassic Period. Its great wings spanned 7 m and it has been calculated that it weighed 16·6 kg. The bony crest on its head looks bulky but in fact was only 3 mm thick and was used for controlling the movement of its head when it was in flight. To give its wings greater strength, the shoulder girdle was fused to the backbone instead of being attached with muscles as it is in most animals. *Pteranodon* had no teeth and no tail: the claws on its wings would have been used for grooming, cleaning parasites from its fur and for holding its mate.

Quetzalcoatlus, a new pterosaur recently discovered in Texas, was even larger than *Pteranodon*, with an estimated wing span of 10 m. It lived inland, soaring over the plains like a vulture, and feeding on carrion.

Pteranodon roosted like a bat on the cliff face. On the ground it moved clumsily, with its wings folded over its back. In the air it was a good flier, snatching fish from the ocean with its beak or gliding from the cliffs to land on the surface.

THE END OF THE DINOSAURS

One of the greatest unsolved mysteries in the history of the earth is the sudden extinction of many groups of animals that took place at the end of the Cretaceous Period, 64 million years ago. All the dinosaurs vanished completely. So did the pterosaurs and the marine reptiles, most shelled cephalopods and several other groups of small animals without backbones.

Scientists have tried to explain this strange event in several ways. Some say that the newly evolving mammals were too intelligent for the small-brained dinosaurs. But in fact the mammals of the time were rather like shrews and hedgehogs and so were not particularly intelligent animals.

Many people believe that the disappearance of the dinosaurs was connected with the spread of modern flowering plants. Before these appeared the plant-eating dinosaurs had fed mainly on conifers, cycads and ferns. All these contain oils that have a laxative effect and when the dinosaurs changed to a diet of flowering plants, with no oils, they would have suffered seriously from constipation. Once the plant eaters were gone, the flesh eaters would have been without food and they, too, would have become extinct. In fact we know that several groups of dinosaurs adapted successfully to a diet of modern plants, so the constipation theory seems unlikely to be correct.

Another theory is that dinosaurs developed a hormone disease which made their eggshells too thick so that the embryos inside could neither breathe nor break out. Still another is that a group of animal egg-eaters developed and ate the eggs faster than the dinosaurs could lay them.

Any of these theories might be right for the dinosaurs alone, but what about the other animals that disappeared at the same time – the pterosaurs, the marine reptiles and the small animals without backbones?

The most recent explanation is connected with the movement of the continents. Since the beginning of the Jurassic the continents had been slowly drifting apart. In the Cretaceous this movement was speeded up. When the great southern continent of Gondwanaland finally split up, the newly formed floor of the ocean was raised up and sea levels rose all over the world. Shallow seas spread over large areas of the land. The sea always has a great influence on climate and now it made temperatures much the same all over the world, from the equator to the poles. These conditions were ideal for animal life, both in the sea and on land and, as we have seen, many different animals evolved during this time.

At the end of the Cretaceous, however, the sea retreated. The climate of the world changed: the polar regions grew much colder and in other places hot and cold seasons developed. In cold winters the dinosaurs' method of controlling their internal temperature would have been positively dangerous. In spite of their size, they would gradually have cooled down as the temperature fell over several months until they were too cold to function properly. When the warmer weather came, they would not have been able to warm up quickly enough to recover.

The changes in climate brought unsettled, stormy weather which the delicate-boned pterosaurs could never have survived. In the seas conditions also changed, affecting the microscopic forms of life floating on the surface waters. This in turn affected the animals which fed on them and the giant marine reptiles which fed on *them*.

One difficulty about this theory is that in some places, for example in northern Nigeria, North America and France, the rocks do not show any evidence of climatic changes during this period: at one particular point in time giant reptiles simply vanished. If there were major climatic changes here, they have left no record.

Though the dinosaurs disappeared, other groups of animals continued to evolve. On land birds, lizards and mammals and in the sea the bony fish all flourished. The Age of Dinosaurs had ended but new animals were ready to take over their place in the world. The future belonged to the birds and the mammals: the Age of Mammals was beginning.

MODERN REPTILES

No dinosaurs survived beyond the end of the Cretaceous, but one of the most successful of all animal groups, the birds, are their only living descendants. The very first bird, *Archaeopteryx*, evolved from the small flesh-eating coelurosaurs in the Jurassic Period, 150 million years ago.

Since the dinosaurs disappeared, reptiles have never again been so important – but this does not mean that they have not been successful. Anyone visiting the tropics cannot help noticing the large number and variety of reptiles there. With the birds, they dominate the forests and savannah regions. Only in the open plains are the mammals supreme.

There are five major groups of living reptiles,

and it is difficult to see what they have in common that enabled them to survive when the dinosaurs vanished. Only one now seems due for extinction: the tuatara lizard *Sphenodon*, which is almost exactly the same as it was in the Triassic, 200 million years ago. It is now found only in remote areas of the South Island of New Zealand, sharing the burrows of sea birds.

Modern lizards were established 150 million years ago in the Jurassic and during their long history they have developed in many different ways. The gliding lizard *Draco*, with its parachuting membrane, is similar to the long extinct glider *Kuehneosaurus*: on the Galapagos islands *Iguana* lizards have returned to the sea and become sea-weed eaters; the slow, stealthy, stalking chameleons that change colour to match their surroundings are another new adaptation.

Perhaps the most remarkable of the living reptiles are the snakes. Their loosely-jointed jaws enable them to swallow animals much bigger than themselves, and they have efficient poisons to prepare their prey for digestion. The first pythons evolved in the Cretaceous and today snakes have adapted successfully to all sorts of different environments.

The last two groups of reptiles are the turtles and tortoises and the crocodiles. Both these appeared in the Triassic and have changed little since, though for a time there were giant forms. Turtles and tortoises live on land, in fresh water and in the sea. They feed on plants and some even catch fish. Individually they are almost indestructible, though turtle eggs are used as food and turtles are hunted by man for their flesh. It has been well said that long after mankind has disappeared from earth, the armoured tortoise will still be here, plodding slowly on its way.

Crocodiles are the only living archosaurs, the group of reptiles to which dinosaurs also belonged. For 200 million years they have remained as semi-aquatic hunters and scavengers. Their only real enemy is man, who is hunting them almost to extinction to make their skin into handbags and shoes. It would be tragic if after surviving for so long, the only living reptilian relative of the dinosaurs were to be destroyed by man.

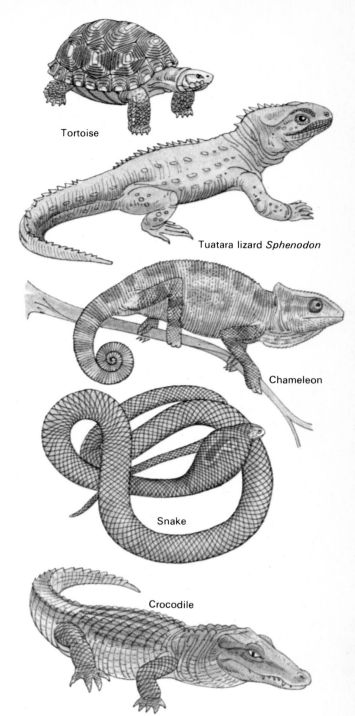

Tortoise

Tuatara lizard *Sphenodon*

Chameleon

Snake

Crocodile

Though the Age of Reptiles ended 64 million years ago, five groups remain: crocodiles, tortoises and turtles, tuatara lizards, modern lizards and snakes. Crocodiles, the only living archosaurs, have remained almost unchanged for 200 million years.

Birds, now classed as a separate group from the reptiles, are the dinosaurs' true descendants: their ancestor, *Archaeopteryx*, evolved from small flesh-eating dinosaurs in the Jurassic Period, 150 million years ago. Today they are among the most successful of all animal groups.

Books for further reading

BAKKER, R T: *Dinosaur Renaissance, Scientific American,* April 1975

BELLAIRS, A d'A and ATTRIDGE, J: *Reptiles,* Hutchinson, London, 1975

CHARIG, A J and HORSFIELD, B: *Before the Ark,* BBC Publications, London 1975

COLBERT, E H: *Dinosaurs, their discovery and their world,* Hutchinson, London, 1961; Dutton, New York, 1961

COLBERT, E H: *Men and Dinosaurs, the search in field and laboratory,* Evans, London, 1968; Dutton, New York, 1968

COX, C B: *Prehistoric Animals,* Paul Hamlyn, London, 1969; Sun Books, Melbourne, 1969

HALSTEAD, L B: *The pattern of vertebrate evolution,* Oliver and Boyd, Edinburgh, 1969; Freeman, San Francisco, 1969

HALSTEAD, L B: *Vertebrate Hard Tissues,* Wykeham Publications, London, 1974; Springer-Verlag, New York, 1974

HALSTEAD, L B and MIDDLETON, J A: *Bare Bones, an exploration in art and science,* Oliver and Boyd, Edinburgh, 1972; University of Toronto Press, Toronto and Buffalo, 1973

KIELAN-JAWOROWSKA, Z: *Hunting for Dinosaurs,* MIT Press, Cambridge, Massachusetts, 1969

ROMER, A S: *Man and the vertebrates,* University of Chicago Press, Chicago, 1933; Penguin Books, Harmondsworth, 1954

STEEL, R: *Die Dinosaurier,* A Ziemsen Verlag, Wittemberg, 1970

SPINAR, Z V and BURIAN, Z: *Life before Man,* Thames and Hudson, London, 1972

SWINTON, W E: *The Dinosaurs,* Allen and Unwin, London, 1970; Wiley, Salt Lake City, 1970

TIME LIFE editors: *Life before Man,* Time-Life International, Amsterdam, 1972

WENDT, H: *Before the Deluge,* Gollancz, London, 1968; Paladin, London, 1970 (paperback)

Glossary

AMPHIBIAN   A vertebrate which lives in the water as a tadpole when young and develops into a land-dwelling, air-breathing adult.

ARCHOSAUR   A major group of reptiles, originally semi-aquatic, which once included the dinosaurs, pterosaurs, birds and crocodiles. Crocodiles are the only remaining archosaurs as birds are now classed separately.

CARAPACE   Armour or covering such as a tortoise's shell.

CEPHALOPOD   Marine MOLLUSC with its foot modified into arms surrounding its mouth, e.g. a squid or octopus. Most shelled cephalopods became extinct 64 million years ago.

COPROLITE   Fossil dropping.

CRUSTACEAN   Shelled animal such as a lobster with many-jointed legs and pincers.

DIGIT   Finger or toe.

EMBRYO   Young developing inside an egg or mother.

FOOD CHAIN   The way in which animals and plants are linked to one another as food, e.g. flesh-eating animals eat plant-eating animals which in turn eat plants.

FOSSIL   Preserved evidence of living things from the past – petrified or mineralized bones, footprints etc.

GENUS (pl. genera)   A grouping of similar SPECIES within a zoological family.

HABITAT   Where an animal lives, its environment.

LAGOON   Enclosed area of sea along coast.

MAMMAL   Warm-blooded, usually furry VERTEBRATE, which suckles its young.

MEMBRANE   A thin sheet of tissue.

METABOLIC RATE   The rate at which food is burned up in the body to produce energy.

MOLLUSC   Soft-bodied, usually shelled animal with large muscular foot, e.g. a snail.

PAVEMENT (of teeth)   Several parallel rows of teeth.

PREDATOR   An animal that preys on others for food.

PREMAXILLA   Tooth-bearing bone at the front of the upper jaw.

PRIMATE   Order of mammals which includes bush-babies, monkeys, apes and man.

PTEROSAUR   A group of warm-blooded, furry flying animals related to dinosaurs but not to birds or bats.

REPTILE   An egg-laying, scaly, air-breathing, cold-blooded vertebrate.

SCAVENGER   An animal that lives by eating up the remains of other animals' kills.

SCUTE   Bony plate in the skin.

SEDIMENT (of rock)   Broken-down rocks carried in small grains by rivers, wind etc.

SEMI-AQUATIC   An animal that spends its life partly in water, partly on land, not necessarily an amphibian.

SERRATED   Notched, like a saw-edge.

SILICA   Silicon dioxide, the mineral that makes up sand and glass, occurring in some plants.

SPECIES   A distinct group of animals which can mate and produce fertile young; a sub-division of genus.

VERTEBRA   Individual bone of backbone.

VERTEBRATE   Animal with a backbone.

Index *Numbers in italics refer to illustrations*

Acknowledgements

The author wishes to thank the following for their kind help: Professor Zofia Kielan-Jaworowska (Warsaw), Dr A.J. Charig and Mr C.A. Walker (British Museum (Natural History) London), Mrs Sandra Collo and Miss Linda Barber. He has referred to recent research papers by Mrs Cherrie Bramwell (pterosaurs); Dr P.M. Galton (*Hypsilophodon*), Mr B.H. Newman (*Tyrannosaurus*), Dr J. Ostrom (hadrosaurs and ceratopsians).

Photographs

The publishers wish to thank the following for permission to reproduce photographs:
British Museum (Natural History) 12–13 (2), 23 (top right), 70, 83
C.M. Dixon 13
L.B. Halstead 17 (right), 23 (below right), 34, 48
Imitor 13
Z. Kielan-Jaworowska 17 (above left, below right), 19 (4), 80, 81
Arnoldo Mondadori Editore 21
Novosti 23 (below left)
Palaontologisches Institüt der Universität Zürich 46
Palaontologisches Museum, Humboldt University, Berlin 66
C.A. Walker 17 (below left)
H.W. Wienert 106